PLAN COOKBOOK FOR BEGINNERS #2020

90+ Easy And Delicious Plant-Based Recipes For A No Meat Lifestyle 30 Day Plant-Based Meal Plan For Radiant Energy And Weight Loss Included

Carla Taylor

Text Copyright ©

All rights reserved. No part of this guide may be reproduced in any form without permission in writing from the publisher except in the case of brief quotations embodied in critical articles or reviews.

Legal & Disclaimer

The information contained in this book and its contents is not designed to replace or take the place of any form of medical or professional advice; and is not meant to replace the need for independent medical, financial, legal or other professional advice or services, as may be required. The content and information in this book has been provided for educational and entertainment purposes only.

The content and information contained in this book has been compiled from sources deemed reliable, and it is accurate to the best of the Author's knowledge, information and belief. However, the Author cannot guarantee its accuracy and validity and cannot be held liable for any errors and/or omissions. Further, changes are periodically made to this book as and when needed. Where appropriate and/or necessary, you must consult a professional (including but not limited to your doctor, attorney, financial advisor or such other professional advisor) before using any of the suggested remedies, techniques, or information in this book.

Upon using the contents and information contained in this book, you agree to hold harmless the Author from and against any damages, costs, and expenses, including any legal fees potentially resulting from the application of any of the information provided by this book. This disclaimer applies to any loss, damages or injury caused by the use and application, whether directly or indirectly, of any advice or information presented, whether for breach of contract, tort, negligence, personal injury, criminal intent, or under any other cause of action.

You agree to accept all risks of using the information presented inside this book.

You agree that by continuing to read this book, where appropriate and/or necessary, you shall consult a professional (including but not limited to your doctor, attorney, or financial advisor or such other advisor as needed) before using any of the suggested remedies, techniques, or information in this book.

Table of contents

INTRODUCTION 9

    WHY YOU NEED TO CUT BACK ON PROCESSED AND ANIMAL-BASED PRODUCTS 11

CHAPTER 1 PLANT-BASED DIET EXPLAINED 15

    KETO DIET 15
    KETOSIS 17
    MACROS 18
    MEAL PREP 19

CHAPTER 2 START TRANSITIONING 21

CHAPTER 3 FULLY TRANSITION 24

CHAPTER 4 UPGRADE THE DIET 27

CHAPTER 5 DEVELOP SUPPORTING HABITS 30

CHAPTER 6 SHOPPING LIST FOR AN EFFECTIVE PLANT-BASED DIET. 34

    WHAT TO AVOID IN A PLANT-BASED DIET 35

CHAPTER 7 RECIPES 37

    BREAKFAST 37
        Keto Porridge 37
        Easy Chia Seed Pudding 38
        Cinnamon Noatmeal 39
        Delicious Vegan Zoodles 40
        Avocado Tofu Scramble 42
        Chia Raspberry Pudding Shots 44
        Healthy Chia-Almond Pudding 45
        Delicious Tofu Fries 46
        Fresh Berries with Cream 48
        Almond Hemp Heart Porridge 49
        Chia Flaxseed Waffles 50
        Cauliflower Zucchini Fritters 52
        Chocolate Strawberry Milkshake 53

Coconut Blackberry Breakfast Bowl 54
Cinnamon Coconut Pancake 55
Flax Almond Muffins 57
Grain-free Overnight Oats 59
Zucchini Muffins 60
Apple Avocado Coconut Smoothie 62
Healthy Breakfast Granola 63
Chia Cinnamon Smoothie 64
Vegetable Tofu Scramble 65
Strawberry Chia Matcha Pudding 66
Healthy Spinach Green Smoothie 67
Avocado Chocó Cinnamon Smoothie 68
Protein Breakfast Shake 69
Avocado Breakfast Smoothie 70
Almond Coconut Porridge 71
MAIN DISHES 72
   burgers 72
   wrap 74
   bowl 76
   hummus 78
   tofu 80
   spaghetti 82
   chilli 83
   fried vegetables 85
   rice 87
   pasta 89
   fajitas 92
   Cauliflower Rice Tabbouleh 94
   Dijon Maple Burgers 96
   Grilled Eggplant Steaks 98
   Cauliflower Steaks 100
   Pesto & Tomato Quinoa 102
   Ratatouille 104
   Olive & Fennel Salad 106
   Baked Okra & Tomato 108
   Cauliflower & Apple Salad 110

Summer Chickpea Salad	112
Edamame Salad	114
Corn & Black Bean Salad	116
Spinach & Orange Salad	117
Fruity Kale Salad	119
Stuffed Bell Pepper	121
SNACKS	123
Zucchini Brownies	123
Tofu Saag	125
Pumpkin & Cinnamon Fudge	127
Oatmeal Sponge Cookies	129
Black Bean Dip	131
Kale Chips	133
Radish Chips	134
Sautéed Pears	135
Pecan & Blueberry Crumble	137
Rice Pudding	139
Mango Sticky Rice	141
SOUP SALADS AND SIDES	143
Cauliflower Coconut Rice	143
Fried Okra	144
Asparagus Mash	145
Baked Asparagus	146
Spinach with Coconut Milk	147
Delicious Cabbage Steaks	148
Garlic Zucchini Squash	149
Tomato Avocado Cucumber Salad	151
Cabbage Coconut Salad	153
Asian Cucumber Salad	154
Mexican Cauliflower Rice	155
Turnip Salad	157
Brussels sprouts Salad	158
Tomato Eggplant Spinach Salad	159
Cauliflower Radish Salad	161
Celery Salad	162
Ginger Avocado Kale Salad	163

Avocado Cabbage Salad 164
  Vegetable Salad 165
  Refreshing Cucumber Salad 167
  Avocado Almond Cabbage Salad 168
 DRINKS AND DESSERT 170
  Avocado Pudding 170
  Almond Butter Brownies 171
  Raspberry Chia Pudding 172
  Chocolate Fudge 173
  Quick Chocó Brownie 174
  Simple Almond Butter Fudge 175
  Coconut Peanut Butter Fudge 176
  Lemon Mousse 177
  Chocó Chia Pudding 178

CHAPTER 8 21-DAY MEAL PLAN 179

CONCLUSION 182

Introduction

Many people have researched and realized that the best to way to adopt a healthier lifestyle is to get into a plant-based diet. This is not an idle statement to make because experts have tried various diets before reaching the conclusion that a plant-based diet is probably the healthiest. These trials have included –

• Fasting intermittently;

• Experimenting with a low carb diet;

• The 6-meals-a-day diet;

• All protein Diet; and

• No sugar diet.

While all these diets have shown merits, a plant-based diet has trumped them all and emerged victorious in all its green and leafy glory. The major benefits of a plant-based diet include a body that is slimmer, stronger, healthier and more energetic. Not just that, because of all the healthy nutrients that the body is getting, a plant-based diet is said to improve life expectancy as well.

Of course, inherently, there are no complications to following this diet. It is simple and easy to incorporate. However, because most people have not grown up with this diet, it is the change that can seem intimidating and might make matters seem more difficult than they actually are.

There is no shame in admitting that change is daunting, and if you are planning to move to a plant-based diet, you're not the only one scared by this change. A little patience and a bit of guidance would help you embrace this diet and welcome your healthier life.

A lot of people are talking about it, but there is still a lot of confusion about what a whole food plant-based diet really means. Because we break food into its macronutrients: carbohydrates, proteins, and fats; most of us get confused about how to eat. What if we could put back together those macronutrients again so that you can free your mind of confusion and stress? Simplicity is the key here.

Whole foods are unprocessed foods that come from the earth. Now, we do eat some minimally processed foods on a whole foods plant-based diet such as whole bread, whole wheat pasta, tofu, non-dairy milk and some nuts and seed butter. All these are fine as long as they are minimally processed. So, here are the different categories:

- Whole grains
- Legumes (basically lentils and beans)
- Fruits and vegetables
- Nuts and seeds (including nut butter)
- Herbs and spices

All the above-mentioned categories make up a whole foods plant-based diet. Where the fun comes in is in how you prepare them; how you season and cook them; and how you mix and match to give them great flavor and variety in your meals. There are chapters in this book dedicated to plant-based recipes which can give you an idea of what you can whip up real quick in your kitchen or those special meals you can prepare for the family.

Now, some people might say, "well, I can't eat soy" or "I don't like tofu" and so on. Well, the beauty of a whole food plant-based diet is that if you don't like a certain food, like in this case, soy, then you don't have to consume it. It is not a necessary component in a whole food plant-based diet. You can have brown rice instead of oats, quinoa instead of wheat; I'm sure you catch the drift now. It doesn't really matter. Just find something that suits you.

Just because you have made the decision to adopt a plant-based diet lifestyle, doesn't mean that is a healthy diet. Plant-based diets have their fair share of junk and other unhealthy eats; case and point, regular consumption of veggie pizzas and non-dairy ice cream. Staying healthy requires you to eat healthy foods – even within a plant-based diet setting.

Why You Need to Cut Back On Processed and Animal-Based Products

You've probably heard time and time again that processed food is bad for you. "Avoid preservatives; avoid processed foods"; however, no one ever really gives you any real or solid information on why you should avoid them and why they are dangerous. So let's break it down so that you can fully understand why you should avoid these culprits.

They have huge addictive properties

As humans, we really have a strong tendency to be addicted to certain foods, but the fact is that it's not entirely our fault.

Practically all of the unhealthy eats we indulge in, from time to time, activate our brains dopamine neurotransmitter. This makes the brain feel "good" but only for a short period of time. This also creates an addiction tendency; that is why someone will always find themselves going back for another candy bar – even though they don't really need it. You can avoid all this by removing that stimulus altogether.

They are loaded sugar and high fructose corn syrup

Processed and animal-based products are loaded with sugars and high fructose corn syrup which have close to zero nutritional value. More and more studies are now proving what a lot of people suspected all along; that genetically modified foods cause gut inflammation which in turn makes it harder for the body to absorb essential nutrients. The downside of your body failing to properly absorb essential nutrients, from muscle loss and brain fog to fat gain, cannot be stressed enough.

They are loaded with refined carbohydrates

Processed foods and animal-based products are loaded with refined carbs. Yes, it is a fact that your body needs carbs to provide energy to run body functions. However, refining carbs eliminates the essential nutrients; in the way that refining whole grains eliminates the whole grain component. What you are left with after refining is what's referred to as "empty" carbs. These can have a negative impact on your metabolism by spiking your blood sugar and insulin levels.

They are loaded with artificial ingredients

When your body is consuming artificial ingredients, it treats them as a foreign object. They essentially become an invader. Your body isn't used to recognizing things like sucralose or these artificial sweeteners. So, your body does what it does best. It triggers an immune response which lowers your resistance making you vulnerable to diseases. The focus and energy spent by your body in protecting your immune system could otherwise be diverted elsewhere.

They contain components that cause a hyper reward sense in your body

What this means is that they contain components like monosodium glutamate (MSG), components of high fructose corn syrup and certain dyes that can actually carve addictive properties. They stimulate your body to get a reward out of it. MSG, for instance, is in a lot of pre-packaged pastries. What this does is that it stimulates your taste buds to enjoy the taste. It becomes psychological just by the way your brain communicates with your taste buds.

This reward-based system makes your body want more and more of it putting you at a serious risk of caloric overconsumption.

What about animal protein? Often times the term "low quality" is thrown around to refer to plant proteins since they tend to have lower amounts of essential amino acids compared to animal protein. What most people do not realize is that more essential amino acids can be quite damaging to your health. So, let's quickly explain how.

Animal Protein Lacks Fiber

In their quest to load up on more animal protein most people end up displacing the plant protein that they already had. This is bad because unlike plant protein, animal protein often lacks in fiber, antioxidants, and phytonutrients. Fiber deficiency is quite common across different communities and societies in the world. In the USA, for instance, according to the Institute of Medicine, the average adult consumes just about 15 grams of fiber per day against the recommended 38 grams. Lack of adequate dietary fiber intake is associated with an increased risk of colon and breast cancers, as well as Crohn's disease, heart disease, and constipation.

Animal protein causes a spike in IGF-1

IGF-1 is the hormone insulin-like growth factor-1. It stimulates cell division and growth, which may sound like a good thing but it also stimulates the growth of cancer cells. Higher blood levels of IGF-1 are thus associated with increased cancer risks, malignancy, and proliferation.

Chapter 1 Plant-based diet explained

The ketogenic plant-based diet is a highly hypocaloric diet with which the amount of different nutrients to be consumed is accurately calculated so that precise proportions between them are respected. Compared to other diets, the percentage of carbohydrates is reduced to around 10%; the proteins are increased only slightly, while the fat intake can reach over 60% of the kilocalories consumed. In this way, the mobilization of the stored fats for energy production and the appearance of a particular metabolic condition called ketosis (or acetonemia), that is an accumulation in the blood of ketone bodies, substances that are formed when using fats to produce power.

This happens even when a person fasts. During fasting, in fact, the body goes through various phases to adapt to the unfavorable situation.

The sugar reserves (glycogen) present in the muscles and the liver are used; when these reserves are over we begin to use proteins, especially those of the muscles, to produce the sugar necessary for survival (through a process called gluconeogenesis); this situation stimulates the body to use fats as a source of energy with a consequent increase in ketone bodies. The ability to adapt to the unfavorable situation of fasting is a very important answer that the body puts in place in case of famine to survive; the brain, in fact, in conditions of lack of sugars, is able to use the ketone bodies to perform its important functions.

keto diet

So you know that the Keto diet is essentially a low-carb, high-fat diet—but you'd be right to wonder just how low is "low-carb?" The traditional map for the Keto diet dictates portions in percentages based on their nutritional source. It looks something like this: eighty-five to ninety percent of your diet should come from whole, healthy fats. After that statistic, you can imagine that there isn't a lot of room for much else. Only six to ten percent of your diet is allowed to consist of protein, while the smallest portion is a tiny two to four percent carbohydrates.

In the meantime, it's incredibly helpful to know which types of foods fit in each area, and what your Keto portions should ideally look like. A typical Keto breakfast can range from steel cut oats, and berries to chocolate protein smoothies. Lunches can be huge colorful salads packed with nuts, berries, and vegetables, while dinners take on hearty spice profiles and creamy vegan sauces to make delicious warm stir-fries and vegetable macaroni. Each modern diet tends to have its own version of the classic food pyramid, but the Keto pyramid is slightly different.

When you think about what to eat on a Keto vegan diet, think about an upside-down pyramid. Your largest and biggest top section is made up of healthy fats and oils—found in nuts, seeds, avocados, and natural oils. Vegetables that aren't too starchy and vegetables that are low in carbohydrates come next, followed by nuts and berries. As a vegan on the Keto diet, you'll want to make sure that almost seventy-five percent of your fats come from plant-based fats, and that your second largest consumption is of low-starch and low-carb vegetables. Vitamins and supplements are definitely the way to go if you haven't already started taking them, but let's look a little closer at the foods you'll want to eat in order to get your nutrients naturally first.

ketosis

As you now know, the human body has a different mechanism for breaking down and refueling that relies on fats and proteins instead of carbohydrates to keep us going. Carbohydrates like starches and fibers are packed full of sugar, and while these can be all-natural sugars, the glucose content in carbohydrate is still much higher than any other food group.

This is where the Ketogenic diet comes into play. Cellular respiration, or the process by which our cells use sugar and oxygen to create carbon dioxide and water, contains a catabolic mechanism that is perfect for breaking down fatty acids. When your body digests healthy, monounsaturated fats, each fat molecule has to be stored in a new form that is designed for later use. Fats are stored as molecules called triglycerides that are made up of one glycerol molecule and three fatty acid tails. Sugars are stored as glycogen. Both glycogen and the fatty acid tails of the stored fat molecules get processed by the Krebs cycle, one of the mechanisms of cellular respiration.

The Krebs cycle consumes acids and water in order to produce molecular bi-products that fuel the next step of energy creation with carbon dioxide as a by-product. Each molecule of stored glucose feeds two molecules of pyruvic acid into the Krebs cycle, which produces three sugar molecules each. This six carbon structure is called citric acid, and it's why the Krebs cycle is also called the Citric Acid cycle. However, something different happens when fat is broken down.

If fatty acids are fed into the Krebs cycle instead of pyruvic acid, they produce thirty-six molecules of sugar per three fatty acid chains in one triglyceride, instead of the six that one glucose molecule produces. While this is a good surplus for our bodies, it's also a surplus that we aren't designed to handle. If you've ever wondered what the

"Ketone" part of the "Keto" diet is, here's the long-awaited answer. Since the Krebs cycle isn't designed to handle so many sugars all at one time, each fatty acid molecule overwhelms the system. Like a bottleneck, the Krebs cycle gets clogged with too many sugar molecules and reverts to changing each excess sugar into a three-part water-soluble Ketone body.

macros

If you haven't already been tracking your "macros and micros" for your regular vegan diet, it's about time that you started. There is no better way to make sure you're getting the exact amount of calories, and the exact amount of nutrients, that your body needs without tracking your macros and micros.

"Macros" is an abbreviation that stands for "macronutrients," and they're what the Keto diet is based on. The three main macronutrients required for human life are carbohydrates, proteins, and fats. That's right! Tracking your macronutrients is just as easy as tracking how many grams of protein, carbohydrates, and fats you're eating in each meal. It does get a bit more complicated than that, but it's nothing you won't be able to handle.

"Micros," then, stands for "micronutrients," and these are quite different from what you might be thinking. Micronutrients are actually the vitamins and minerals that your body requires to function, and micros are often essential for macros to do their jobs. Without the help of certain minerals, our macronutrients wouldn't be able to synthesize new proteins, add in our cellular regeneration, and help move bad molecules like harmful cholesterol out of our arteries. In order to make sure you're getting your proper dosages of micronutrients, you take supplements! One of the many helpful connections between veganism and the Keto diet is that both tend to require a healthy amount of added vitamins and minerals.

meal prep

A vegan Keto diet isn't the **most** restrictive diet out there, but it's certainly one of the more admirable challenges in the health and fitness world. Sticking to a vegan Keto diet can be hard, but meal prepping the best vegan Keto meals will make a world of difference when it comes to upholding your commitment. Many of our lives are constantly busy, and when you're trying to maintain a Keto diet, it's imperative that you eat at the same time each day—especially if you're on a fast. This might mean eating at work or packing a meal to take with you for after the gym.

Either way, preparing your necessary meals each week will give you more time to focus on your mental health and less time worrying about pounds that will melt off naturally. You'll also be able to portion out your carbs, fats, and proteins according to your Keto guidelines, which will help infinitely in organizing. As a vegan eating Keto, you'll also want to make sure that you're paying special attention to things like generated plastic waste—if you're trying to save the planet by eating less meat, it doesn't make much sense to package your snacks each day in disposable Ziploc baggies.

Glass Tupperware are the cornerstones of vegan meal prep containers, and the many different sizes and tight lids of Mason jars are perfect for taking your snacks and salads on the go. But meal preparation is more than just saving you time, money, and precious calories. Portioning out your meals is a key part of both veganism and the Keto diet because of your need to more urgently check certain nutrition boxes.

These nutrition boxes are called you macronutrients and micronutrients, and if fats, carbs, and proteins thought they were the only reason we portioned out or meals, they were very wrong. Tracking your "macros and micros" is just like making sure you don't eat too much bread in one day—except for your body, it's a lot more serious. These essential chemicals can sometimes mean the difference between a perfectly healthy body, and one that struggles to function.

Chapter 2 Start Transitioning

As you enter into the seventh day of the plant-based diet, you need to take steps to fully transition to the diet. This way, you'll have enough time to reap the benefits of the diet. Thus, you should:

Get rid of other meats

Yes, you need to stop eating meat. Remember, you are now on the plant-based diet. The keyword in that diet happens to be 'plant'. This means that your focus should be on eating plant foods. So every other meat, including poultry, fish, pork and others is off limits starting from the 7th day.

Analyze your eating habits

You need to pay attention to your eating habits. If you have bad eating habits, you need to put a stop to them. Some of these bad habits include:

- Eating in front of the television
- Eating whenever you watch a movie
- Eating while working, reading or chatting
- Eating while traveling
- Eating out of a box
- Eating out of a bowl
- Not taking time to chew your food
- Not putting your fork down between bites
- 'Snacking' late at night
- Eating junk food

Instead, you should make it a habit to sit down at the table whenever you want to eat a meal. Focus on the food you're eating and remember to take your time between each bite. Also, you need to pay attention to the composition of your plate. As already stated, your meal needs to include vegetables, fruit, whole foods and protein. This is a complete meal that you can easily get from plant foods.

Make herbs and spices your friends

Herbs and spices can change the way you view certain foods. They bring about a different taste, color and texture to foods. This makes food more interesting and appealing. As a matter of fact, you can use different herbs and spices to create different tastes of the same food. For example, if you love rice, you can cook it with beet root or turmeric or coconut oil and so forth to create various 'types' of rice. As a result, you can enjoy the same food in different flavors. Thus way, you'll never get bored with the food you eat on the plant-based diet. You can use herbs and spices such as basil, curry, turmeric, rosemary and black pepper.

What to expect: After 10 days

The first 10 days of the diet set the foundation for the rest of the 40 days of plant-based diet program. At this point, you should have given up meat, developed good eating habits and changed the composition of your plate.

So, what can you expect after embarking on the plant-based diet?

Well, the first thing you should expect is some resistance to change. Here's the thing. When you have the option to eat meat, you often don't think much about it. You know you can have it whenever you want to. As such, you can easily go without it for days. But when you take away that option, you suddenly realize just how much you 'like' meat. You want it simply because you can no longer have it. When you start craving meat, you need to remind yourself that the sole purpose of eating meat is to get your fair share of protein. You can get this share from plant-based foods. Thus, you'll be alright if you forego meat for 40 days.

Next, you should expect to lose some weight and become more energetic. Yes, the results of switching to a plant-based diet can often be experienced within a few days. But don't expect to see drastic changes. The plant-based diet still involves eating food. The foods you eat can help you lose weight or cause you to gain weight. This is why you need to take into account the composition of your plate. The plant-based diet is not an excuse to overeat. It is supposed to provide healthier food options. But if you eat more calories than you use, you'll end up gaining weight instead of losing it.

Another thing you should expect is to take more frequent trips to the bathroom. This is due to the fact that you'll be eating more fruits and vegetables. Such foods happen to be rich in fiber and higher in water content. Thus, if you previously suffered from things such as constipation, you should expect to get rid of that issue.

Chapter 3 Fully Transition

Getting rid of meat is the first step in fully transitioning to a plant-based diet. But there are other things you still need to do. Remember, your goal is to fully transition to a plant-based diet as soon as you can. This will give your body enough time to adjust to the diet and you'll be able to see the benefits of sticking to the diet. As such, you need to:

Get rid of eggs and dairy

A lot of people think that giving up dairy is the one thing that can stop them from embracing a plant-based diet. But it can be done. Think about it. Less than 40% of adults have the ability to digest lactose. If you can't digest lactose, you'll be faced with issues such as flatulence, bloating, diarrhea, cramping and nausea. This is because the sugars you consume will get stuck in the colon and they will begin to ferment. As such, you have added reason to stop consuming dairy.

Another thing you need to stop eating is eggs. Yes, this includes the eggs you use in baking. Instead of using eggs, you can use things such as flax eggs, banana and chia eggs.

Rethink how you shop

Now that you've gotten rid of meat, eggs and dairy, it is time to rethink how you shop. Start by clearing out your pantry. Get rid of any food product that should not be consumed in the plant-based diet. Next, think of what you need to purchase and where you're likely to get it. Instead of browsing the supermarket isles, you may need to change tactics and head to the farmers markets and farms whenever possible. This way, you'll get fresh produce at lower prices. Don't waste time on things you can no longer eat. Avoid such sections if you can. A list of what you need will come in handy.

You also need to familiarize yourself with the practice of checking labels. Remember, you are now on the plant-based diet. Animal products should not have a place in your shopping list. Reading labels will help you see any red flags and as such, you'll be able to avoid such products.

Stock your pantry

You should make it a habit to stock your pantry with the types of food you want to eat. As they say, out of sight, out of mind. If you want to add certain foods in your diet, you need to be able to reach for them whenever you need them. Foods such as fruits, vegetables, whole grains, healthy fats, legumes, nuts and seeds should all have a place in your pantry. It would certainly help to have a few recipes nearby so that you can plan for what you'll need to buy.

Don't go overboard when you are shopping. You don't need to stock your pantry with foods you won't eat. It would be wiser to find a few foods you intend to use frequently and make sure you have enough of them. For example, you can shop in bulk for things such as rice and oats and decide to shop weekly for things such as fresh fruits and vegetables. As time goes by, you'll have a good idea of how much food you'll be eating and your shopping will become easier.

What to expect: After 20 days

In the first two weeks, you should have fully transitioned to the plant-based diet. After 20 days, you can check your progress to see if you are on the right track. There are certain things you'll notice after 20 days on the plant-based diet.

Once you fully switch to the plant-based diet, you should expect to have bad days. Yes, there are days that will be more difficult than others. This is especially so in the first few days of fully transitioning. You'll crave certain foods. You'll crave animal products and start 'dreaming about' foods you can no longer eat. This is normal. But as days go by, the cravings will subside. Something else that you'll notice is that your taste buds will 'come alive'. The various foods you'll be eating will contribute to a boost in taste and sensation. You need to give yourself time to adjust before determining whether or not you like a certain type of food.

On a positive note, you'll soon notice that you have a lot of energy. This energy will be consistent throughout the day. It won't fluctuate. Things like afternoon 'slumps' will be things of the past. If you were used to sleeping in the course of the day, you'll find that you are more alert throughout the day. As such, your days will become more productive. If you take advantage of this, you'll be able to experience improved sleep during the night.

Once you give up eggs and dairy, you'll notice a change in how you feel. If your body was constantly experiencing aches and pains, you'll find relief. This is because the foods you'll be eating will be full of anti-inflammatory properties. They will help you get rid of chronic pain.

As you fully embrace the diet, you may find yourself fielding questions from your friends and family. People will be curious and some will be suspicious as they see the changes you are making. They will have questions and some may discourage you and make fun of you. This should not stop you from completing the program. This is the time to remind yourself of your motivations and while you're on it, you need to learn to upgrade the diet.

Chapter 4 Upgrade The Diet

It's normal to feel anxious when you start following the plant-based diet. You want to get it right and quickly get rid of the things you should not be eating. That's well and good. But once you transition to the diet, you need to find ways to fully take advantage of it. You can do this by 'upgrading the diet'. By this, this is what I mean:

Eat whole foods

One way to upgrade your plant-based diet is to start using whole foods. Processed foods are obviously bad for you. By the time they come out of the factory, they are turned into something that is hardly recognizable and that has no nutritional value to you. Instead of eating such products, you'd do well to buy whole foods. You can buy things such as brown rice, faro, barley, rolled oats and brown rice pasta. It may take some time for you to get accustomed to such foods but they are definitely worth it. Whole foods increase the quality of your diet. They come with extra nutrients and antioxidants. In other words, they are healthy and they are good for you.

You should also think seriously about getting rid of wheat and wheat products. Yes, wheat is plant-based but this does not mean that it is good for you. If you feel 'funny' after consuming wheat products, you shouldn't ignore such feelings. You may not have major issues with gluten but you'll notice a difference once you stop consuming such products.

Make substitutions

There are a lot of food products you will be giving up. You may want to make substitutions for such products. This will remove the temptation of using products you shouldn't be using. For example, instead of using milk, you can use unsweetened milks such as almond, cashew and coconut milk. Such milks bring in a different flavor and they will ensure you get your fair amount of nutrients such as calcium. You can also add plant-based proteins to your diet instead of using meat. You can use plant proteins such as tofu and tempeh.

Of course, making food substitutions will lead to new discoveries. You may need to find different ways of cooking. This can be adventurous to you. Make it fun. Set aside two days a week to discover something new. This will keep you interested in the diet and you'll get to know the plant-based foods you prefer.

Cook ahead

You can save yourself a lot of heartache by cooking ahead. Things such as beans and other legumes can be prepared ahead. This way, you'll always have a source of protein whenever you want to eat a balanced meal. It's prudent to cook ahead especially when the foods you want to use take several hours to cook. If you don't cook ahead, you'll find it difficult to stick to the diet. On the other hand, if you cook ahead, you can plan for the week and determine how to get what you need from the diet.

All in all, you want to make it easier for yourself to go on the plant-based diet and to stick to it.

What to expect: After 30 days

After 30 days on the plant-based diet, you should expect to see significant changes. If you have a 'before' photo, you'll be surprised at the changes that have occurred as they will be 'obvious'. Of course, you should expect to lose weight. After all, you have been eating more fruits and vegetables and getting an adequate share of carbs and healthy protein. There's one thing you need to know about such foods. They make you full. When you consume healthy foods, you should expect to lose weight. You should expect to become leaner as the 'pockets of fat' disappear.

You should also expect to have clearer skin. You'll experience 'skin glow' as your skin becomes healthier. Your hair and your nails will also benefit from the plant-based diet. Your hair should become shinier and your nails should become stronger. Don't be surprised when people around you comment on the 'new' you. The changes of the diet will be visible to all around you.

You should also be able to experience a boost in focus, stamina and endurance. Your libido should also benefit from the diet. A plant-based diet is meant to energize you throughout the day. This means that you'll benefit both mentally and physically. You'll be able to do more things simply because you are thinking more clearly and you have more energy. In the midst of all this, it is important that you develop supporting habits that will enable you to stick to the diet.

Chapter 5 Develop Supporting Habits

Starting the plant-based diet is recommendable. But it would be better if you complete the 40 days of plant-based diet program. Some people have the tendency to go back to old ways once they experience positive changes in their health. They start feeling good and start thinking that all their problems have been solved. They forget that the reason they were experiencing such problems in the first place was due to the fact that they had formed bad eating habits. This needs not be the case. You can develop supporting habits that will allow you to fully embrace the plant-based diet. These include:

At restaurants, ask

It is one thing to embrace the plant-based diet in the safety of your home but what happens when you eat out? Do you 'forget' about the diet? Do you take that as an opportunity to 'cheat' on the diet? You don't need to. You can make a habit of asking about the ingredients. There are many restaurants that are plant-based diet friendly. You should find out where you can eat and which foods are safe to eat in other restaurants. Sauces and condiments may contain animal products. As such, if you don't know the contents of such products, you need to ask.

What about when you socialize with friends?

Well, a plant-based diet is not meant to restrict your fun. You can still meet up with friends and socialize with them. The only difference is that you'll need to be more cautious of the food that is served.

Cook at home

It's also good to cook at home most of the time. This is because doing so gives you greater freedom when it comes to choosing your ingredients. You can determine what to use at any given time. You can ensure that all the products you use are plant based. Instead of eating out, you can prepare your lunch at home and carry it with you as you go about your day. Cooking at home will also ensure that you keep your food costs down. As such, you should get some cookbooks and recipes and put them to good use. Take note of the foods you like and the recipes you'll want to try again. These will form the base of your diet. If you have 4-5 go-to recipes, you can build the rest of your diet from there. You don't need a variety of recipes; just several of them that you can use frequently.

Practice mindfulness

Mindfulness is one practice that everyone should adopt. When you are mindful, you'll no longer brush things aside. You'll be forced to look at what you are doing and live each moment fully. This means that you'll take note of the food you are eating. You'll think about what it takes to place it on your plate. You'll think about how it came to be and the process that allowed you to actually get that food. You'll think about what it takes to prepare that food and the people involved in the preparation. As such, you'll learn to appreciate every bite you eat.

Mindfulness is concerned with living your life in the moment. A lot of people don't take time to fully appreciate the food they eat. This is not right. You need to enjoy your food. You need to chew it properly and give your attention to it. You need to notice the taste, the smell and the texture of food instead of just swallowing it quickly. Mindfulness will help you slow down your eating and this will enable you to fully grasp the importance of eating healthy foods.

Respect others

You can make it a point to alert your friends about your diet. This will ensure that they provide options whenever you visit them. If they have questions, make sure you answer them in a way that will explain your position without attacking them. Remember, it is just food. You can't eat all types of food in the world. But you can determine which foods you can actually eat. Once you do, don't make a big issue out of it. Live your life and allow others to make their own choices.

What to expect: After 40 days

Once you go through the 40 days of plant-based diet program, you should expect to have a healthy, energetic and youthful body. This is not a myth. The food you eat determines the health of your body. A plant-based diet gets rid of inflammation and pain. It reduces the risk of getting diseases such as heart disease and diabetes. It keeps you focused and energetic. Above all, a plant-based diet increases your happiness. This is because you'll be happy knowing that you are doing the right thing where your health is concerned. You'll also be happy to note that by eating a plant-based diet, you are actually contributing to saving the environment.

But there's something else you need to consider.

You need to consider what you'll do once you are through with the plant-based program. One thing you need to note is that there is no one way to embrace the plant-based diet. As a matter of fact, there are various plant-based diets you can try out. Some of them allow you to eat things such as fish and dairy. It's up to you to determine what you're comfortable with and the changes you are willing to live with. One good way to make your decisions is by re-introducing some foods to your diet and noting down how they make you feel. If you are uncomfortable with such foods, stop eating them. You don't need them.

Your health is of utmost importance. Therefore, make sure to make changes that will benefit you and lead to a healthier, more energetic and youthful you. Let's now look at some of the recipes you can use on the plant-based diet.

Chapter 6 Shopping list for an effective plant-based diet.

Basically, in a plant-based diet, you eat plants and only plants. There is an elimination of animal products and that includes dairy but don't be scared because this guide will help you make the change gradually without pressure.

There are many plant-based foods that people are not used to eating in their daily lives. These foods have hence fallen off the radar of most people and only the popular plant products come to mind when you think about a plant-based diet. Also, this is another factor that might put you off this diet because you think that there are only a handful of plant related products that you can eat. You are wrong because there is this a huge section of plants that are edible, delicious and you have no idea about them. For example, here is a list of plants products, some of which you may have heard but most of which would be unknown to you –

- Tofu
- Broccoli
- Tempeh
- Seitan
- Kale
- Quinoa
- Chia seeds (ground)
- Flaxseeds (ground)

- Walnuts

- Raw almonds

- Butter of raw almonds

- Black beans

- Hemp seeds

- Spirulina

- Organic soymilk

- Nutritional yeast

- Flourless sprouted bread

- Steel cut oats

- Brown rice

The ultimate plant-based diet is also known by the term "veganism" and although, some plant-based dieters do include certain animal products, the best and the healthiest option is going vegan.

What to avoid in a plant-based diet

Meat: All kinds of meat products such as fish, seafood, poultry, red meat, and even processed meat products are not allowed in a plant-based diet.

Eggs: You can't eat eggs, as it contains high cholesterol content.

Dairy: All forms of dairy products are not accepted in this diet. You have to avoid milk, yogurt, cream, cheese, buttermilk, and half-and-half.

Vegan replacements: Vegan replacements of meats and cheese are also not allowed. Such replacements contain high oil content, which is not acceptable in the plant-based diet.

Added fat: You have to say no to all kinds of added fats such as coconut oil, butter, margarine, and all other liquid oils.

Refined flours: Any flour that is not 100% in terms of whole wheat is not accepted. You can't use refined flours in your diet.

Added sugar: Any food item with added flavoring or sugar is not allowed. Along with that, you have to say no to energy bars, candy bars, cakes, cookies, and all other junk food options.

Beverages: In the category of beverages, you can't have soda or even fruit juices. Even the fruit juices with 100% purity are not allowed. At the same time, you are recommended to stay away from energy drinks, sports drinks, tea drinks, blended coffee, and other harmful beverages that contain flavorings or high-sugar content.

Chapter 7 Recipes

Breakfast

Keto Porridge

Total Time: 10 minutes

Serves: 1

Ingredients:

- ½ tsp vanilla extract
- ¼ tsp granulated stevia
- 1 tbsp chia seeds
- 1 tbsp flaxseed meal
- 2 tbsp unsweetened shredded coconut
- 2 tbsp almond flour
- 2 tbsp hemp hearts
- ½ cup water
- Pinch of salt

Directions:

- Add all ingredients except vanilla extract to a saucepan and heat over low heat until thickened.
- Stir well and serve warm.

Nutritional Value (Amount per Serving): Calories 370; Fat 30.2 g; Carbohydrates 12.8 g; Sugar 1.9 g; Protein 13.5 g; Cholesterol 0 mg;

Easy Chia Seed Pudding

Total Time: 10 minutes

Serves: 4

Ingredients:

- ¼ tsp cinnamon
- 15 drops liquid stevia
- ½ tsp vanilla extract
- ½ cup chia seeds
- 2 cups unsweetened coconut milk

Directions:

- Add all ingredients into the glass jar and mix well.
- Close jar with lid and place in refrigerator for 4 hours.
- Serve chilled and enjoy.

Nutritional Value (Amount per Serving): Calories 347; Fat 33.2 g; Carbohydrates 9.8 g; Sugar 4.1 g; Protein 5.9 g; Cholesterol 0 mg;

Cinnamon Noatmeal

Total Time: 10 minutes

Serves: 2

Ingredients:

- ¾ cup hot water
- 2 tbsp sugar-free maple syrup
- ½ tsp ground cinnamon
- 2 tbsp ground flax seeds
- 3 tbsp vegan vanilla protein powder
- 3 tbsp hulled hemp seeds

Directions:

- Add all ingredients into the bowl and stir until well combined.
- Serve and enjoy.

Nutritional Value (Amount per Serving): Calories 220; Fat 12.5 g; Carbohydrates 9.5 g; Sugar 0.1 g; Protein 17.6 g; Cholesterol 0 mg;

Delicious Vegan Zoodles

Total Time: 15 minutes

Serves: 4

Ingredients:

- 4 small zucchinis, spiralized into noodles
- 3 tbsp vegetable stock
- 1 cup red pepper, diced
- 1/2 cup onion, diced
- 3/4 cup nutritional yeast
- 1 tbsp garlic powder
- Pepper
- Salt

Directions:

- Add zucchini noodles, red pepper, and onion in a pan with vegetable stock and cook over medium heat for few minutes.
- Add nutritional yeast and garlic powder and cook for few minutes until creamy.
- Season with pepper and salt.
- Stir well and serve.

Nutritional Value (Amount per Serving): Calories 71; Fat 0.9 g; Carbohydrates 12.1 g; Sugar 5.7 g; Protein 5.7 g; Cholesterol 0 mg;

Avocado Tofu Scramble

Total Time: 15 minutes

Serves: 1

Ingredients:

- 1 tbsp fresh parsley, chopped
- ½ medium avocado
- ½ block firm tofu, drained and crumbled
- ½ cup bell pepper, chopped
- ½ cup onion, chopped
- 1 tsp olive oil
- 1 tbsp water
- ¼ tsp cumin
- ¼ tsp garlic powder
- ¼ tsp paprika
- ¼ tsp turmeric
- 1 tbsp nutritional yeast
- Pepper
- Salt

Directions:

- Heat olive oil to the pan over medium heat.
- Add onion and bell pepper and sauté for 5 minutes.
- Add crumbled tofu and nutritional yeast to the pan and sauté for 2 minutes.
- Top with parsley and avocado.
- Serve and enjoy.

Nutritional Value (Amount per Serving): Calories 164; Fat 9.7 g; Carbohydrates 15 g; Sugar 6 g; Protein 7.4 g; Cholesterol 0 mg;

Chia Raspberry Pudding Shots

Total Time: 10 minutes

Serves: 4

Ingredients:

- ½ cup raspberries
- 10 drops liquid stevia
- 1 tbsp unsweetened cocoa powder
- ¼ cup unsweetened almond milk
- ½ cup unsweetened coconut milk
- ¼ cup chia seeds

Directions:

- Add all ingredients into the glass jar and stir well to combine.
- Pour pudding mixture into the shot glasses and place in refrigerator for 1 hour.
- Serve chilled and enjoy.

Nutritional Value (Amount per Serving): Calories 117; Fat 10 g; Carbohydrates 5.9 g; Sugar 1.7 g; Protein 2.7 g; Cholesterol 0 mg;

Healthy Chia-Almond Pudding

Total Time: 10 minutes

Serves: 2

Ingredients:

- ½ tsp vanilla extract
- ¼ tsp almond extract
- 2 tbsp ground almonds
- 1 ½ cups unsweetened almond milk
- ¼ cup chia seeds

Directions:

- Add chia seeds in almond milk and soak for 1 hour.
- Add chia seed and almond milk into the blender.
- Add remaining ingredients to the blender and blend until smooth and creamy.
- Serve and enjoy.

Nutritional Value (Amount per Serving): Calories 138; Fat 10.2 g; Carbohydrates 6 g; Sugar 0.5 g; Protein 5.1 g; Cholesterol 0 mg;

Delicious Tofu Fries

Total Time: 50 minutes

Serves: 4

Ingredients:

- 15 oz firm tofu, drained, pressed and cut into long strips
- ¼ tsp garlic powder
- ¼ tsp onion powder
- ¼ tsp cayenne pepper
- ¼ tsp paprika
- ½ tsp oregano
- ½ tsp basil
- 2 tbsp olive oil
- Pepper
- Salt

Directions:

- Preheat the oven to 190 C/ 375 F.
- Add all ingredients into the large mixing bowl and toss well.
- Place marinated tofu strips on a baking tray and bake in preheated oven for 20 minutes.
- Turn tofu strips to other side and bake for another 20 minutes.
- Serve and enjoy.

Nutritional Value (Amount per Serving): Calories 137; Fat 11.5 g; Carbohydrates 2.3 g; Sugar 0.8 g; Protein 8.8 g; Cholesterol 0 mg;

Fresh Berries with Cream

Total Time: 10 minutes

Serves: 1

Ingredients:

- 1/2 cup coconut cream
- 1 oz strawberries
- 1 oz raspberries
- 1/4 tsp vanilla extract

Directions:

- Add all ingredients into the blender and blend until smooth.
- Pour in serving bowl and top with fresh berries.
- Serve and enjoy.

Nutritional Value (Amount per Serving): Calories 303; Fat 28.9 g; Carbohydrates 12 g; Sugar 6.8 g; Protein 3.3 g; Cholesterol 0 mg;

Almond Hemp Heart Porridge

Total Time: 10 minutes

Serves: 2

Ingredients:

- ¼ cup almond flour
- ½ tsp cinnamon
- ¾ tsp vanilla extract
- 5 drops stevia
- 1 tbsp chia seeds
- 2 tbsp ground flax seed
- ½ cup hemp hearts
- 1 cup unsweetened coconut milk

Directions:

- Add all ingredients except almond flour to a saucepan. Stir to combine.
- Heat over medium heat until just starts to lightly boil.
- Once start bubbling then stir well and cook for 1 minute more.
- Remove from heat and stir in almond flour.
- **Serve immediately and enjoy.**

Nutritional Value (Amount per Serving): Calories 329; Fat 24.4 g; Carbohydrates 9.2 g; Sugar 1.8 g; Protein 16.2 g; Cholesterol 0 mg;

Chia Flaxseed Waffles

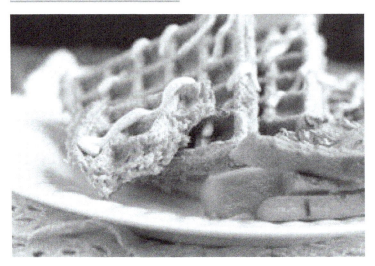

Total Time: 25 minutes

Serves: 8

Ingredients:

- 2 cups ground golden flaxseed
- 2 tsp cinnamon
- 10 tsp ground chia seed
- 15 tbsp warm water
- 1/3 cup coconut oil, melted
- 1/2 cup water
- 1 tbsp baking powder
- 1 tsp sea salt

Directions:

- Preheat the waffle iron.
- In a small bowl, mix together ground chia seed and warm water.

- In a large bowl, mix together ground flax seed, sea salt, and baking powder. Set aside.
- Add melted coconut oil, chia seed mixture, and water into the blender and blend for 30 seconds.
- Transfer coconut oil mixture into the flax seed mixture and mix well. Add cinnamon and stir well.
- Scoop waffle mixture into the hot waffle iron and cook on each side for 3-5 minutes.
- Serve and enjoy.

Nutritional Value (Amount per Serving): Calories 240; Fat 20.6 g; Carbohydrates 12.9 g; Sugar 0 g; Protein 7 g; Cholesterol 0 mg;

Cauliflower Zucchini Fritters

Total Time: 15 minutes

Serves: 4

Ingredients:

- 3 cups cauliflower florets
- ¼ tsp black pepper
- ¼ cup coconut flour
- 2 medium zucchini, grated and squeezed
- 1 tbsp coconut oil
- ½ tsp sea salt

Directions:

- Steam cauliflower florets for 5 minutes.
- Add cauliflower into the food processor and process until it looks like rice.
- Add all ingredients except coconut oil to the large bowl and mix until well combined.
- Make small round patties from the mixture and set aside.
- Heat coconut oil in a pan over medium heat.
- Place patties on pan and cook for 3-4 minutes on each side.
- **Serve and enjoy.**

Nutritional Value (Amount per Serving): Calories 68; Fat 3.8 g; Carbohydrates 7.8 g; Sugar 3.6 g; Protein 2.8 g; Cholesterol 0 mg;

Chocolate Strawberry Milkshake

Total Time: 5 minutes

Serves: 2

Ingredients:

- 1 cup ice cubes
- ¼ cup unsweetened cocoa powder
- 2 scoops vegan protein powder
- 1 cup strawberries
- 2 cups unsweetened coconut milk

Directions:

- Add all ingredients into the blender and blend until smooth and creamy.
- Serve immediately and enjoy.

Nutritional Value (Amount per Serving): Calories 221; Fat 5.7 g; Carbohydrates 15 g; Sugar 6.8 g; Protein 27.7 g; Cholesterol 0 mg;

Coconut Blackberry Breakfast Bowl

Total Time: 10 minutes

Serves: 2

Ingredients:

- 2 tbsp chia seeds
- ¼ cup coconut flakes
- 1 cup spinach
- ¼ cup water
- 3 tbsp ground flaxseed
- 1 cup unsweetened coconut milk
- 1 cup blackberries

Directions:

- Add blackberries, flaxseed, spinach, and coconut milk into the blender and blend until smooth.
- Fry coconut flakes in pan for 1-2 minutes.
- Pour berry mixture into the serving bowls and sprinkle coconut flakes and chia seeds on top.
- Serve immediately and enjoy.

Nutritional Value (Amount per Serving): Calories 182; Fat 11.4 g; Carbohydrates 14.5 g; Sugar 4.3 g; Protein 5.3 g; Cholesterol 0 mg;

Cinnamon Coconut Pancake

Total Time: 15 minutes

Serves: 1

Ingredients:

- 1/2 cup almond milk
- 1/4 cup coconut flour
- 2 tbsp egg replacer
- 8 tbsp water
- 1 packet stevia
- 1/8 tsp cinnamon
- 1/2 tsp baking powder
- 1 tsp vanilla extract
- 1/8 tsp salt

Directions:

- In a small bowl, mix together egg replacer and 8 tablespoons of water.

- Add all ingredients into the mixing bowl and stir until combined.
- Spray pan with cooking spray and heat over medium heat.
- Pour the desired amount of batter onto hot pan and cook until lightly golden brown.
- Flip pancake and cook for a few minutes more.
- Serve and enjoy.

Nutritional Value (Amount per Serving): Calories 110; Fat 4.3 g; Carbohydrates 10.9 g; Sugar 2.8 g; Protein 7 g; Cholesterol 0 mg;

Flax Almond Muffins

Total Time: 45 minutes

Serves: 6

Ingredients:

- 1 tsp cinnamon
- 2 tbsp coconut flour
- 20 drops liquid stevia
- 1/4 cup water
- 1/4 tsp vanilla extract
- 1/4 tsp baking soda
- 1/2 tsp baking powder
- 1/4 cup almond flour
- 1/2 cup ground flax
- 2 tbsp ground chia

Directions:

- Preheat the oven to 350 F/ 176 C.
- Spray muffin tray with cooking spray and set aside.
- In a small bowl, add 6 tablespoons of water and ground chia. Mix well and set aside.

- In a mixing bowl, add ground flax, baking soda, baking powder, cinnamon, coconut flour, and almond flour and mix well.
- Add chia seed mixture, vanilla, water, and liquid stevia and stir well to combine.
- Pour mixture into the prepared muffin tray and bake in preheated oven for 35 minutes.
- Serve and enjoy.

Nutritional Value (Amount per Serving): Calories 92; Fat 6.3 g; Carbohydrates 6.9 g; Sugar 0.4 g; Protein 3.7 g; Cholesterol 0 mg;

Grain-free Overnight Oats

Total Time: 10 minutes

Serves: 1

Ingredients:

- 2/3 cup unsweetened coconut milk
- 2 tsp chia seeds
- 2 tbsp vanilla protein powder
- ½ tbsp coconut flour
- 3 tbsp hemp hearts

Directions:

- Add all ingredients into the glass jar and stir to combine.
- Close jar with lid and place in refrigerator for overnight.
- Top with fresh berries and serve.

Nutritional Value (Amount per Serving): Calories 378; Fat 22.5 g; Carbohydrates 15 g; Sugar 1.5 g; Protein 27 g; Cholesterol 0 mg;

Zucchini Muffins

Total Time: 35 minutes

Serves: 8

Ingredients:

- 1 cup almond flour
- 1 zucchini, grated
- 1/4 cup coconut oil, melted
- 15 drops liquid stevia
- 1/2 tsp baking soda
- 1/2 cup coconut flour
- 1/2 cup walnut, chopped
- 1 1/2 tsp cinnamon
- 3/4 cup unsweetened applesauce
- 1/8 tsp salt

Directions:

- Preheat the oven to 325 F/ 162 C.
- Spray muffin tray with cooking spray and set aside.

- In a bowl, combine together grated zucchini, coconut oil, and stevia.
- In another bowl, mix together coconut flour, baking soda, almond flour, walnut, cinnamon, and salt.
- Add zucchini mixture into the coconut flour mixture and mix well.
- Add applesauce and stir until well combined.
- Pour batter into the prepared muffin tray and bake in preheated oven for 25-30 minutes.
- Serve and enjoy.

Nutritional Value (Amount per Serving): Calories 229; Fat 18.9 g; Carbohydrates 12.5 g; Sugar 3.4 g; Protein 5.2 g; Cholesterol 0 mg;

Apple Avocado Coconut Smoothie

Total Time: 5 minutes

Serves: 2

Ingredients:

- 1 tsp coconut oil
- 1 tbsp collagen powder
- 1 tbsp fresh lime juice
- ½ cup unsweetened coconut milk
- ¼ apple, slice
- 1 avocado

Directions:

- Add all ingredients into the blender and blend until smooth and creamy.
- Serve and enjoy.

Nutritional Value (Amount per Serving): Calories 262; Fat 23.9 g; Carbohydrates 13.6 g; Sugar 3.4 g; Protein 2 g; Cholesterol 0 mg;

Healthy Breakfast Granola

Total Time: 15 minutes

Serves: 5

Ingredients:

- 1 cup walnuts, diced
- 1 cup unsweetened coconut flakes
- 1 cup sliced almonds
- 2 tbsp coconut oil, melted
- 4 packets Splenda
- 2 tsp cinnamon

Directions:

- Preheat the oven to 375 F/ 190 C.
- Spray a baking tray with cooking spray and set aside.
- Add all ingredients into the medium bowl and toss well.
- Spread bowl mixture on a prepared baking tray and bake in preheated oven for 10 minutes.
- Serve and enjoy.

Nutritional Value (Amount per Serving): Calories 458; Fat 42.5 g; Carbohydrates 13.7 g; Sugar 2.7 g; Protein 11.7 g; Cholesterol 0 mg;

Chia Cinnamon Smoothie

Total Time: 5 minutes

Serves: 1

Ingredients:

- 2 scoops vanilla protein powder
- 1 tbsp chia seeds
- ½ tsp cinnamon
- 1 tbsp coconut oil
- ½ cup water
- **½ cup unsweetened coconut milk**

Directions:

- Add all ingredients into the blender and blend until smooth and creamy.
- **Serve immediately and enjoy.**

Nutritional Value (Amount per Serving): Calories 397; Fat 23.9 g; Carbohydrates 13.4 g; Sugar 0 g; Protein 31.6 g; Cholesterol 0 mg;

Vegetable Tofu Scramble

Total Time: 20 minutes

Serves: 2

Ingredients:

- 1 block firm tofu, drained and crumbled
- ½ tsp turmeric
- ¼ tsp garlic powder
- 1 cup spinach
- 1 red pepper, chopped
- 10 oz mushrooms, chopped
- ½ onion, chopped
- 1 tbsp olive oil
- Pepper
- Salt

Directions:

- Heat olive oil in a large pan over medium heat.
- Add onion, pepper, and mushrooms and sauté until cooked.
- Add crumbled tofu, spices, and spinach. Stir well and cook for 3-5 minutes.
- Serve and enjoy.

Nutritional Value (Amount per Serving): Calories 159; Fat 9.6 g; Carbohydrates 13.7 g; Sugar 7 g; Protein 9.6 g; Cholesterol 0 mg;

Strawberry Chia Matcha Pudding

Total Time: 10 minutes

Serves: 1

Ingredients:

- 5 drops liquid stevia
- 2 strawberries, diced
- 1 ½ tbsp chia seeds
- ¾ cup unsweetened coconut milk
- ½ tsp matcha powder

Directions:

- Add all ingredients except strawberries into the glass jar and mix well.
- Close jar with lid and place in refrigerator for 4 hours.
- Add strawberries into the pudding and mix well.
- Serve and enjoy.

Nutritional Value (Amount per Serving): Calories 93; Fat 6.5 g; Carbohydrates 5.6 g; Sugar 1.2 g; Protein 2.5 g; Cholesterol 0 mg;

Healthy Spinach Green Smoothie

Total Time: 5 minutes

Serves: 1

Ingredients:

- 1 cup ice cube
- 2/3 cup water
- ½ cup unsweetened almond milk
- 5 drops liquid stevia
- ½ tsp matcha powder
- 1 tsp vanilla extract
- 1 tbsp MCT oil
- ½ avocado
- 2/3 cup spinach

Directions:

- Add all ingredients into the blender and blend until smooth and creamy.
- Serve immediately and enjoy.

Nutritional Value (Amount per Serving): Calories 167; Fat 18.3 g; Carbohydrates 3.8 g; Sugar 0.6 g; Protein 1.6 g; Cholesterol 0 mg;

Avocado Chocó Cinnamon Smoothie

Total Time: 5 minutes

Serves: 1

Ingredients:

- ½ tsp coconut oil
- 5 drops liquid stevia
- ¼ tsp vanilla extract
- 1 tsp ground cinnamon
- 2 tsp unsweetened cocoa powder
- ½ avocado
- ¾ cup unsweetened coconut milk

Directions:

- Add all ingredients into the blender and blend until smooth and creamy.
- Serve immediately and enjoy.

Nutritional Value (Amount per Serving): Calories 95; Fat 8.3 g; Carbohydrates 5.1 g; Sugar 0.2 g; Protein 1.2 g; Cholesterol 0 mg;

Protein Breakfast Shake

Total Time: 10 minutes

Serves: 2

Ingredients:

- 1 cup coconut milk, unsweetened
- 1 scoop protein powder
- 7 oz firm tofu
- 15 drops liquid stevia
- 1 tbsp cocoa powder
- 1 tbsp cocoa nibs
- 1 tbsp chia seeds
- 2 tbsp hemp hearts
- 1/2 oz almonds

Directions:

- Add all ingredients into the blender and blend until you get a thick consistency.
- Serve and enjoy.

Nutritional Value (Amount per Serving): Calories 243; Fat 13 g; Carbohydrates 11 g; Sugar 1.4 g; Protein 21.2 g; Cholesterol 23 mg;

Avocado Breakfast Smoothie

Total Time: 5 minutes

Serves: 2

Ingredients:

- 5 drops liquid stevia
- ¼ cup ice cubes
- ½ avocado
- 1 tsp vanilla extract
- 1 cup unsweetened coconut milk

Directions:

- Add all ingredients into the blender and blend until smooth and creamy.
- Serve immediately and enjoy.

Nutritional Value (Amount per Serving): Calories 131; Fat 11.8 g; Carbohydrates 5.6 g; Sugar 0.5 g; Protein 1 g; Cholesterol 0 mg;

Almond Coconut Porridge

Total Time: 10 minutes

Serves: 2

Ingredients:

- ¾ cup unsweetened almond milk
- ½ tsp vanilla extract
- 1 ½ tbsp ground flaxseed
- 3 tbsp ground almonds
- 6 tbsp unsweetened shredded coconut
- Pinch of sea salt

Directions:

- Add almond milk in microwave safe bowl and microwave for 2 minutes.
- Add remaining ingredients and stir well and cook for 1 minute.
- Top with fresh berries and serve.

Nutritional Value (Amount per Serving): Calories 197; Fat 17.4 g; Carbohydrates 8.3 g; Sugar 0.6 g; Protein 4.2 g; Cholesterol 0 mg;

Main dishes

burgers

Serves: 6

Time: 25 Minutes

Calories: 173

Protein: 7.3 Grams

Fat: 3.2 Grams

Carbs: 29.7 Grams

Ingredients:

- 1 Onion, Diced
- ½ Cup Corn Nibs
- 2 Cloves Garlic, Minced
- ½ Teaspoon Oregano, Dried
- ½ Cup Flour
- 1 Jalapeno Pepper, Small
- 2 Cups Black Beans, Mashed & Canned
- ¼ Cup Breadcrumbs (Vegan)

- 2 Teaspoons Parsley, Minced
- ¼ Teaspoon Cumin
- 1 Tablespoon Olive Oil
- 2 Teaspoons Chili Powder
- ½ Red Pepper, Diced
- Sea Salt to Taste

Directions:

1. Set your flour on a plate, and then get out your garlic, onion, peppers and oregano, throwing it in a pan. Cook over medium-high heat, and then cook until the onions are translucent. Place the peppers in, and sauté until tender.
2. Cook for two minutes, and then set it to the side.
3. Use a potato masher to mash your black beans, and then stir in the vegetables, cumin, breadcrumbs, parsley, salt and chili powder, and then divide it into six patties.
4. Coat each side, and then cook until it's fried on each side.

Interesting Facts: Potatoes are a great starchy source of potassium and protein. They are pretty inexpensive if you are one that is watching their budget. Bonus: Very heart healthy!

wrap

Serves: 1

Time: 10 Minutes

Calories: 428

Protein: 13 Grams

Fat: 23 Grams

Carbs: 47 Grams

Ingredients:

- ¼ Cup Crispy Chickpeas
- ¼ Cup Cherry Tomatoes, Halved
- Handful Baby Spinach
- 2 Romaine Lettuce Leaves for Wrapping
- 2 Tablespoons Lemon Juice, Fresh
- ¼ Cup Hummus
- 2 Tablespoons Kalamata Olives, Quartered

Directions:
1. Mix everything but your lettuce leaves and hummus together.
2. Put your hummus on your lettuce leaves, topping with your chickpea mixture, and then serve immediately.

Interesting Facts: Chickpeas are highly versatile and can easily be utilized in a vast array of dishes. They are infamous for making delicious hummus! They are loaded with 6 grams of protein per serving, and they are easy. You can also use chickpea water as an egg replacement known as aquafaba!

bowl

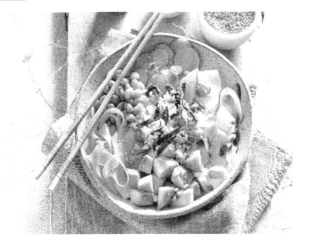

Serves: 1

Time: 40 Minutes

Calories: 467

Protein: 22 Grams

Fat: 20 Grams

Carbs: 56 Grams

Ingredients:

- ½ Cup Edamame Beans, Shelled & Fresh
- ¾ Cup Brown Rice, Cooked
- ½ Cup Spinach, Chopped
- ¼ Cup Bell Pepper, Sliced
- ¼ Cup Avocado, Sliced
- ¼ Cup Cilantro, Fresh & Chopped
- 1 Scallion, Chopped
- ¼ Nori Sheet
- 1-2 Tablespoons Tamari

- 1 Tablespoon Sesame Seeds, Optional

Directions:
1. Steam your edamame beans, and then assemble your edamame, rice, avocado, spinach, cilantro, scallions and bell pepper into a bowl.
2. Cut the nori into ribbons, sprinkling it on top, drizzling with tamari and sesame seeds before serving.

Interesting Facts: Avocados are known as miracle fruits in the world of Veganism. They are a true super-fruit and incredibly beneficial. They are one of the best things to eat if you are looking to incorporate more fatty acids in your diet. They are also loaded with 20 various minerals and vitamins. Plus, they are easy to incorporate into dishes all throughout the day!

hummus

Serves: 4

Time: 5 Minutes

Calories: 150

Protein: 8 Grams

Fat: 4 Grams

Carbs: 23 Grams

Ingredients:

- 1 Can Butter Beans, Drained & Rinsed
- 4 Sprigs Parsley, Minced
- 1 Tablespoon Olive Oil
- ½ Lemon, Juiced
- 2 Cloves Garlic, Minced
- Sea Salt to Taste

Directions:

1. Blend and serve as a dip with fresh vegetables.

Interesting Facts: This oil is a main source of dietary fat in a variety of diets. It contains many vitamins and minerals that play a part in reducing the risk of stroke and lowers cholesterol and high blood pressure and can also aid in weight loss. It is best consumed cold, as when it is heated it can lose some of its nutritive properties (although it is still great to cook with – extra virgin is best), many recommend taking a shot of cold oil olive daily! Bonus: if you don't like the taste or texture add a shot to your smoothie.

tofu

Serves: 4

Time: 30 Minutes

Calories: 262

Protein: 16 Grams

Fat: 15 Grams

Carbs: 19 Grams

Ingredients:

- ¾ Cup Scallions, Sliced Thin
- 1 ½ Tablespoons Mirin
- ¼ Cup Tamari
- 1 ½ Tablespoon Dark Sesame Oil, Toasted
- 1 Tablespoon Sesame Seeds, Toasted (Optional)
- 2 Teaspoons Ginger, fresh & Grated
- ½ Teaspoon Red Pepper, crushed
- 12 Ounces Extra Firm Tofu, Drained & Cut into ½ Inch Pieces

- 4 Cups Zucchini Noodles
- 2 Tablespoons Rice Vinegar
- 2 Cups Carrots, Shredded
- 2 Cups Pea Shoots
- ¼ Cup Basil, Fresh & Chopped
- ¼ Cup Peanuts, Toasted & Chopped (Optional)

Directions:

1. Wisk your tamari, mirin, sesame seeds, oil, ginger, red pepper, and scallion greens in a bowl. Set two tablespoons of this sauce aside, and add the tofu to the remaining sauce. Toss to coat.
2. Combine your vinegar and zucchini noodles in a bowl.
3. Divide it between four bowls, topping with tofu, carrots, and a tablespoon of basil and peanuts.
4. Drizzle with sauce before serving.

Interesting Facts: Sesame seeds can be easily added to crackers, bread, salads, and stir-fry meals. Bonus: Help in lowering cholesterol and high blood pressure. Double bonus: Help with asthma, arthritis, and migraines!

spaghetti

Serves: 24

Time: 45 Minutes

Calories: 138

Protein: 1.5 Grams

Fat: 4.8 Grams

Carbs: 21.9 Grams

Ingredients;

- 1 ½ Cups Vegan Sugar
- 1 Teaspoon Baking Soda
- 1 Teaspoon Sea Salt, Fine
- ½ Cup Cocoa, Unsweetened
- 2 Tablespoons Vanilla Extract, Pure
- ½ Cup Oil
- 2 Cups Zucchini, Peeled & Grated

Directions:

1. Mix your cocoa, salt, flour, sugar and baking soda together.
2. Add in your oil, vanilla and zucchini, mixing well.
3. Bake at 350 in a nine by thirteen inch pan until done.

Interesting Facts: The recipe is great to use as a substitute for spaghetti/noddles, just grab a spiralizer and get spiralizing!

chilli

Serves: 4

Time: 30 Minutes

Calories: 160

Protein: 8 Grams

Fat: 3 Grams

Carbs: 29 Grams

Ingredients:

- 1 Onion, Diced
- 1 Teaspoon Olive Oil
- 3 Cloves Garlic, Minced
- 28 Ounces Tomatoes, Canned
- ¼ Cup Tomato Paste
- 14 Ounces Kidney Beans, Canned, Rinsed & Dried
- 2-3 Teaspoons Chili Powder
- ¼ Cup Cilantro, Fresh (or Parsley)
- ¼ Teaspoon Sea Salt, Fine

Directions:
1. Get out a pot, and sauté your onion and garlic in your oil at the bottom cook for five minutes. Add in your tomato paste, tomatoes, beans, and chili powder. Season with salt.
2. Allow it to simmer for ten to twenty minutes.
3. Garnish with cilantro or parsley to serve.

Interesting Facts: Kidney beans are packed with Vitamin B6, potassium, folate, and fiber. Every serving has 7.6 grams of protein. They can easily be used to make yummy veggie burgers, vegan brownies or a killer vegan Mexican meal!

fried vegetables

Serves: 4

Time: 30 Minutes

Calories: **95**

Protein: 1 Gram

Fat: 7 Grams

Carbs: 10 Grams

Ingredients:

- 2 Tablespoons Olive Oil
- 3 Cups Vegetable Broth
- 2 Tablespoons Lemon Juice, Fresh
- ½ Teaspoon Garlic Powder
- ½ Cup Carrots, Shredded
- 2 Cups Cabbage, Shredded
- 1 Cup Beets, Shredded
- Dill for Garnish
- ½ Teaspoon Onion Powder

- Sea Salt & Black Pepper to Taste

Directions:
1. Heat oil in a pot, and then sauté your vegetables.
2. Pour your broth in, mixing in your seasoning. Simmer until it's cooked through, and then top with dill.

Interesting Facts: This oil is a main source of dietary fat in a variety of diets. It contains many vitamins and minerals that play a part in reducing the risk of stroke and lowers cholesterol and high blood pressure and can also aid in weight loss. It is best consumed cold, as when it is heated it can lose some of its nutritive properties (although it is still great to cook with – extra virgin is best), many recommend taking a shot of cold oil olive daily! Bonus: if you don't like the taste or texture add a shot to your smoothie.

rice

Serves: 6

Time: 1 Hour 35 Minutes

Calories: 330

Protein: 5 Grams

Fat: 10 Grams

Carbs: 52 Grams

Ingredients:

- 1 Cup Brown Rice
- 1 Teaspoon Vanilla Extract, Pure
- ½ Teaspoon Sea Salt, Fine
- ½ Teaspoon Cinnamon
- ¼ Teaspoon Nutmeg
- 3 Egg Substitutes

- 3 Cups Coconut Milk, Light
- 2 Cups Brown Rice, Cooked

Directions:
1. Blend all of your ingredients together before pouring them into a two quarter dish.
2. Bake at 300 for ninety minutes before serving.

Interesting Facts: Brown rice is incredibly high in antioxidants and good vitamins. It's relative, 14 white rice is far less beneficial as much of these healthy nutrients get destroyed during the process of milling. You can also opt for red and black rice or wild rice. The meal options for this healthy grain are limitless!

pasta

Total Preparation & Cooking time: 30 mins.

Servings: 4

Ingredients

- 1/3 cup roasted peanuts, dry & chopped
- 8 oz. whole wheat spaghetti, uncooked
- 1 and 1/2 tbsp. soy sauce, low sodium
- 3 tbsp. creamy peanut butter
- 1/4 tsp. red pepper flakes, crushed or 1/4 tsp. hot chili sauce
- 1 tsp. garlic, minced
- 1/4 cup teriyaki sauce, low-sodium
- 2 tbsp. hot water
- 1 bag frozen vegetables (approximately 16 oz. stir fry variety)
- 2 tbsp. soy sauce or 2 tbsp. teriyaki sauce
- 1 extra firm tofu, water-packed (approximately 16 oz. & drained)
- 2 tsp. sesame oil

Directions

1. Place tofu among a number of paper towels layers (preferably heavy-duty) and prepare the tofu. Cover tofu with some more paper towels, pressing occasionally and let the tofu stand approximately 5 minutes.

2. Cut the tofu into ½" cubes and then place the tofu in a bowl. Add either teriyaki sauce or soy sauce, and toss well to coat the tofu completely. Cover; chill for a minimum period of an hour.

3. Cook the pasta according to directions mentioned on the package, omitting fat and salt; drain and keep it aside.

4. Combine hot water, teriyaki sauce, red pepper flakes (or hot Chile sauce), and peanut butter, stirring with a whisk.

5. Over medium-high heat in a large nonstick skillet, heat the sesame oil. Add the minced garlic and sauté approximately a minute.

6. Add the tofu with the pasta and sauté until tofu has browned a little, approximately 5 minutes.

7. Add the teriyaki sauce mixture & cook approximately 2 to 3 minutes.

8. Add soy sauce, vegetables, and pasta; cook until heated thoroughly, stirring well.

9. Remove the pasta from the heat & sprinkle peanuts over it.

Nutritional Value (Amount Per Serving): 553.6 Calories, 23.3 g Total Fat, 0 mg Cholesterol, 68.7 g Total Carbohydrate, 7.1 g Dietary Fiber, 27.9 g Protein

fajitas

Serves: 4

Time: 13 Minutes

Calories: 76

Protein: 4.4 Grams

Fat: 2.7 Grams

Carbs: 9.8 Grams

Ingredients:

- 1 Head Bok Choy
- 1 Teaspoon Canola Oil
- 1/3 Cup Green Onion, Chopped
- 1 Tablespoon Brown Sugar
- 1 ½ Tablespoon Soy Sauce, Light
- 1 Tablespoon Rice Wine
- ½ Teaspoon Ginger, Ground
- 1 Tablespoon Sesame Seeds

Directions:
1. Cut the stems and tops of your bok choy into one inch pieces.
2. Mix together all remaining ingredients in a bowl.
3. Add your bok choy, and top with your dressing.
4. Fry until tender, which should take eight to ten minutes.

Interesting Facts: Sesame seeds can be easily added to crackers, bread, salads, and stir-fry meals. Bonus: Help in lowering cholesterol and high blood pressure. Double bonus: Help with asthma, arthritis, and migraines!

Cauliflower Rice Tabbouleh

Serves: 4

Time: 20 Minutes

Calories: **220**

Protein: 7 Grams

Fat: 15 Grams

Carbs: 20 Grams

Ingredients:

- 4 Cups Cauliflower Rice
- 1 ½ Cups Cherry Tomatoes, Quartered
- 3-4 Tablespoons Olive Oil
- 1 Cup Parsley, Fresh & Chopped
- 1 Cup Mint, Fresh & Chopped
- 1 Cup Snap Peas, Sliced Thin
- 1 Small Cucumber, Cut into ¼ Inch Pieces
- ¼ Cup Scallions, Sliced Thin
- 3-4 Tablespoons Lemon Juice, Fresh
- 1 Teaspoon Sea Salt, Fine

- ½ Teaspoon Black Pepper

Directions:

1. Get out a bowl and combine your cauliflower rice, tomatoes, mint, parsley, cucumbers, scallions and snap peas together. Toss until combined.
2. Add your olive oil and lemon juice before tossing again. Season with salt and pepper.

Interesting Facts: Cauliflower: This vegetable is an extremely high source of vitamin A, vitamin B1, B2 and B3.

Dijon Maple Burgers

Serves: 12

Time: 50 Minutes

Calories: 200

Protein: 8 Grams

Fat: 11 Grams

Carbs: 21 Grams

Ingredients:

- 1 Red Bell Pepper
- 19 Ounces Can Chickpeas, Rinsed & Drained
- 1 Cup Almonds, Ground
- 2 Teaspoons Dijon Mustard
- 1 Teaspoon Oregano
- ½ Teaspoon Sage

- 1 Cup Spinach, Fresh
- 1 – ½ Cups Rolled Oats
- 1 Clove Garlic, Pressed
- ½ Lemon, Juiced
- 2 Teaspoons Maple Syrup, Pure

Directions:

1. Get out a baking sheet. Line it with parchment paper.
2. Cut your red pepper in half and then take the seeds out. Place it on your baking sheet, and roast in the oven while you prepare your other ingredients.
3. Process your chickpeas, almonds, mustard and maple syrup together in a food processor.
4. Add in your lemon juice, oregano, sage, garlic and spinach, processing again. Make sure it's combined, but don't puree it.
5. Once your red bell pepper is softened, which should roughly take ten minutes, add this to the processor as well. Add in your oats, mixing well.
6. Form twelve patties, cooking in the oven for a half hour. They should be browned.

Interesting Facts: Spinach is one of the most superb green veggies out there. Each serving is packed with 3 grams of protein and is a highly encouraged component of the plant-based diet.

Grilled Eggplant Steaks

Serves: 6

Time: 35 Minutes

Calories: 86

Protein: 8 Grams

Fat: 7 Grams

Carbs: 12 Grams

Ingredients:

- 4 Roma Tomatoes, Diced
- 8 Ounces Feta, Diced
- 2 Eggplants
- 1 Tablespoon Olive Oil
- 1 Cup Parsley, Chopped
- 1 Cucumber, Diced
- Sea Salt & Black Pepper to Taste

Directions:

1. Slice your eggplants into three thick steaks, and then drizzle with oil. Season then grill for four minutes per side in a pan.
2. Top with the remaining ingredients.

Interesting Facts: Eggplant has a variety of vital vitamins and minerals within it's compound. It is high in folic acid, vitamin C, manganese and vitamin K. It aids weight lose and cognitive function. Eggplant is a great meat replacement in a lasagna!

Cauliflower Steaks

Serves: 4

Time: 30 Minutes

Calories: 167

Protein: 6 Grams

Fat: 13 Grams

Carbs: 10 Grams

Ingredients:

- ¼ Teaspoon Black Pepper
- ½ Teaspoon Sea Salt, Fine
- 1 Tablespoon Olive Oil
- 1 Head Cauliflower, Large
- ¼ Cup Creamy Hummus
- 2 Tablespoons Lemon Sauce
- ½ Cup Peanuts, Crushed (Optional)

Directions:
1. Start by heating your oven to 425.
2. Cut your cauliflower stems, and then remove the leaves. Put the cut side down, and then slice half down the middle. Cut into ¾ inch steaks. If you cut them thinner, they could fall apart.
3. Arrange them in a single layer on a baking sheet, drizzling with oil. Season and bake for twenty to twenty-five minutes. They should be lightly browned and tender.
4. Spread your hummus on the steaks, drizzling with your lemon sauce. Top with peanuts if you're using it.

Interesting Facts: Cauliflower: This vegetable is an extremely high source of vitamin A, vitamin B1, B2 and B3.

Pesto & Tomato Quinoa

Serves: 1

Time: 25 Minutes

Calories: 535

Protein: 20 Grams

Fat: 23 Grams

Carbs: 69 Grams

Ingredients:

- 1 Teaspoon Olive Oil
- 1 Cup Onion, Chopped
- 1 Cup Zucchini, Chopped
- 1 Clove Garlic, Minced
- 1 Tomato, Chopped
- Pinch Sea Salt
- 2 Tablespoons Sun Dried Tomatoes, Chopped
- 2-3 Tablespoons Basil Pesto
- 1 Cup Spinach, Chopped
- 2 Cups Quinoa, Cooked
- 1 Tablespoon Nutritional Yeast, Optional

Directions:
1. Heat your oil in a skillet, and sauté your onion over medium-high heat. This should take five minutes, and then add in your garlic, cooking for another minute. Add in your sea salt and zucchini.
2. Cook for about five-minute and then add in your sun dried tomatoes, and mix well.
3. Toss your pesto in, and then mix well.
4. Layer your spinach, quinoa and then zucchini mixture on a plate, topping with nutritional yeast if desired.

Interesting Facts: Quinoa is an important staple for anyone looking to get the most out of a plant-based diet.

Ratatouille

Serves: 10

Time: 1 Hour 15 Minutes

Calories: 90

Protein: 3 Grams

Fat: 25 Grams

Carbs: 13 Grams

Ingredients:

- 2 Tablespoons Olive Oil
- 2 Eggplants, Peeled & Cubed
- 8 Zucchini, Chopped
- 4 Tomatoes, Chopped
- ¼ Cup Basil, Chopped
- 4 Thyme Sprigs
- 2 Yellow Onions, Diced
- 3 Cloves Garlic, Minced
- 3 Bell Peppers, Chopped
- 1 Bay Leaf

- Sea Salt to Taste

Directions:
1. Salt your eggplant and leave it in a strainer.
2. Heat a teaspoon of oil in a Dutch oven, cooking your onions for ten minutes. Season with salt.
3. Mix your peppers in, cooking for five more minutes.
4. Place this mixture in a bowl.
5. Heat your oil and sauté zucchini, sprinkling with salt. Cook for five minutes, and place it in the same bowl.
6. Rinse your eggplant, squeezing the water out, and heat another two teaspoons of oil in your Dutch oven. Cook your eggplant for ten minutes, placing it in your vegetable bowl.
7. Heat the remaining oil and cook your garlic. Add in your tomatoes, thyme sprigs and bay leaves to deglaze the bottom.
8. Toss your vegetables back in, and then bring it to a simmer.
9. Simmer for forty-five minutes, and make sure to stir. Discard your thyme and bay leaf. Mix in your basil and serve warm.

Interesting Facts: Eggplant has a variety of vital vitamins and minerals within it's compound. It is high in folic acid, vitamin C, manganese and vitamin K. It aids weight lose and cognitive function. Eggplant is a great meat replacement in a lasagna!

Olive & Fennel Salad

Serves: 3

Time: 5 Minutes

Calories: 331

Protein: 3 Grams

Fat: 29 Grams

Carbs: 15 Grams

Ingredients:

- 6 Tablespoons Olive Oil
- 3 Fennel Bulbs, Trimmed, Cored & Quartered
- 2 Tablespoons Parsley, Fresh & Chopped
- 1 Lemon, Juiced & Zested
- 12 Black Olives
- Sea Salt & Black Pepper to Taste

Directions:

1. Grease your baking dish, and then place your fennel in it. Make sure the cut side is up.
2. Mix your lemon zest, lemon juice, salt, pepper and oil, pouring it over your fennel.
3. Sprinkle your olives over it, and bake at 400.
4. Serve with parsley.

Interesting Facts: This oil is a main source of dietary fat in a variety of diets. It contains many vitamins and minerals that play a part in reducing the risk of stroke and lowers cholesterol and high blood pressure and can also aid in weight loss. It is best consumed cold, as when it is heated it can lose some of its nutritive properties (although it is still great to cook with – extra virgin is best), many recommend taking a shot of cold oil olive daily! Bonus: if you don't like the taste or texture add a shot to your smoothie.

Baked Okra & Tomato

Serves: 6

Time: 1 Hour 15 Minutes

Calories: 55

Protein: 3 Grams

Fat: 0 Grams

Carbs: 12 Grams

Ingredients:

- ½ cup Lime Beans, Frozen
- 4 Tomatoes, Chopped
- 8 Ounces Okra, Fresh, Washed & Stemmed, Sliced into ½ Inch Thick Slices
- 1 Onion, Sliced into Rings
- ½ Sweet Pepper, Seeded & Sliced Thin
- Pinch Crushed Red Pepper
- Sea Salt to taste

Directions:

1. Start by heating the oven to 350, and then cook your lime beans. Drain them, and then get out a two-quarter casserole.
2. Combine everything together, and bake covered with foil for fort-five minutes.
3. Stir, and then uncover. Bake for another thirty minutes, and stir before serving.

Interesting Facts: These beans are another great multi-use veggie. They are packed with Vitamin B6, potassium, folate, and fiber. Every serving has 7.6 grams of protein. They can easily be used to make yummy veggie burgers, vegan brownies or a killer vegan Mexican meal!

Cauliflower & Apple Salad

Serves: 4

Time: 25 Minutes

Calories: 198

Protein: 7 Grams

Fat: 8 Grams

Carbs: 32 Grams

Ingredients:

- 3 Cups Cauliflower, Chopped into Florets
- 2 Cups Baby Kale
- 1 Sweet Apple, Cored & Chopped
- ¼ Cup Basil, Fresh & Chopped
- ¼ Cup Mint, Fresh & Chopped
- ¼ Cup Parsley, Fresh & Chopped
- 1/3 Cup Scallions, Sliced Thin

- 2 Tablespoons Yellow Raisins
- 1 Tablespoon Sun Dried Tomatoes, Chopped
- ½ Cup Miso Dressing, Optional
- ¼ Cup Roasted Pumpkin Seeds, Optional

Directions:

1. Combine everything together, tossing before serving.

Interesting Facts: This vegetable is an extremely high source of vitamin A, vitamin B1, B2 and B3.

Summer Chickpea Salad

Serves: 4

Time: 15 Minutes

Calories: 145

Protein: 4 Grams

Fat: 7.5 Grams

Carbs: 16 Grams

Ingredients:

- 1 ½ Cups Cherry Tomatoes, Halved
- 1 Cup English Cucumber, Slices
- 1 Cup Chickpeas, Canned, Unsalted, Drained & Rinsed
- ¼ Cup Red Onion, Slivered
- 2 Tablespoon Olive Oil
- 1 ½ Tablespoons Lemon Juice, Fresh
- 1 ½ Tablespoons Lemon Juice, Fresh
- Sea Salt & Black Pepper to Taste

Directions:

1. Mix everything together, and toss to combine before serving.

Interesting Facts: Chickpeas are highly versatile and can easily be utilized in a vast array of dishes. They are infamous for making delicious hummus! They are loaded with 6 grams of protein per serving, and they are easy. You can also use chickpea water as an egg replacement known as aquafaba!

Edamame Salad

Serves: 1

Time: 15 Minutes

Calories: 299

Protein: 20 Grams

Fat: 9 Grams

Carbs: 38 Grams

Ingredients:

- ¼ Cup Red Onion, Chopped
- 1 Cup Corn Kernels, Fresh
- 1 Cup Edamame Beans, Shelled & Thawed
- 1 Red Bell Pepper, Chopped
- 2-3 Tablespoons Lime Juice, Fresh
- 5-6 Basil Leaves, Fresh & Sliced
- 5-6 Mint Leaves, Fresh & Sliced
- Sea Salt & Black Pepper to Taste

Directions:

1. Place everything into a Mason jar, and then seal the jar tightly. Shake well before serving.

Interesting Facts: Whole corn is a fantastic source of phosphorus, magnesium, and B vitamins. It also promotes healthy digestion and contains heart-healthy antioxidants. It is important to seek out organic corn in order to bypass all of the genetically modified product that is out on the market.

Corn & Black Bean Salad

Salad: 6

Time: 10 Minutes

Calories: 159

Protein: 6.4 Grams

Fat: 5.6 Grams

Carbs: 23.7 Grams

Ingredients:

- ¼ Cup Cilantro, Fresh & Chopped
- 1 Can Corn, Drained (10 Ounces)
- 1/8 Cup Red Onion, Chopped
- 1 Can Black Beans, Drained (15 Ounces)

- 1 Tomato, Chopped
- 3 Tablespoons Lemon Juice, Fresh
- 2 Tablespoons Olive Oil
- Sea Salt & Black Pepper to Taste

Directions:

1. Mix everything together, and then refrigerate until cool. Serve cold.

Interesting Facts: Whole corn is a fantastic source of phosphorus, magnesium, and B vitamins. It also promotes healthy digestion and contains heart-healthy antioxidants. It is important to seek out organic corn in order to bypass all of the genetically modified product that is out on the market.

Spinach & Orange Salad

Serves: 6

Time: 15 Minutes

Calories: 99

Protein: 2.5 Grams

Fat: 5 Grams

Carbs: 13.1 Grams

Ingredients:

- ¼ -1/3 Cup Vegan Dressing
- 3 Oranges, Medium, Peeled, Seeded & Sectioned
- ¾ lb. Spinach, Fresh & Torn
- 1 Red Onion, Medium, Sliced & Separated into Rings

Directions:

1. Toss everything together, and serve with dressing.

Interesting Facts: Spinach is one of the most superb green veggies out there. Each serving is packed with 3 grams of protein and is a highly encouraged component of the plant-based diet.

Fruity Kale Salad

Serves: 4

Time: 30 Minutes

Calories: 220

Protein: 4 Grams

Fat: 17 Grams

Carbs: 16 Grams

Ingredients:

Salad:
- 10 Ounces Baby Kale
- ½ Cup Pomegranate Arils
- 1 Tablespoon Olive Oil
- 1 Apple, Sliced

Dressing:
- 3 Tablespoons Apple Cider Vinegar
- 3 Tablespoons Olive Oil

- 1 Tablespoon Tahini Sauce (Optional)
- Sea Salt & Black Pepper to Taste

Directions:

1. Wash and dry the kale. If kale is too expensive, you can also use lettuce, arugula or spinach. Take the stems out, and chop it.
2. Combine all of your salad ingredients together.
3. Combine all of your dressing ingredients together before drizzling it over the salad to serve.

Interesting Facts: Kale is the latest superfood of the Vegan world. It is a favorite when deciding to eliminate meat from your diet as it is very high in iron, vitamin K and potassium. It is also extremely high in fibre and vitamin A.

Stuffed Bell Pepper

Serves: 4

Time: 25 Minutes

Calories: 126

Protein: 3 Grams

Fat: 5 Grams

Carbs: 19 Grams

Ingredients:

- 4 Bell Peppers, Halved & Hollowed
- ½ Cup Quinoa, Cooked
- 12 Black Olives, Halved
- 1/3 Cup Tomatoes, Sun Dried
- ½ Cup Baby Spinach
- 2 Cloves Garlic, Minced
- Sea Salt & Black Pepper to Taste

Directions:

1. Bake your peppers at 400 for ten minutes, and then mix the rest of your ingredients in a bowl.
2. Stuff your peppers with the quinoa mixture.

Interesting Facts: Quinoa: Although it is actually a seed, we treat it mainly as a grain in the way in which it is prepared. This South American gem has an incredible amount of protein and therefore can serve as a great substitute for meat products. Quinoa is an important staple for anyone looking to get the most out of a plant-based diet.

Snacks

Zucchini Brownies

Serves: 24

Time: 45 Minutes

Calories: 138

Protein: 1.5 Grams

Fat: 4.8 Grams

Carbs: 21.9 Grams

Ingredients;

- 2 Cups Flour
- 1 ½ Cups Vegan Sugar
- 1 Teaspoon Baking Soda
- 1 Teaspoon Sea Salt, Fine
- ½ Cup Cocoa, Unsweetened
- 2 Tablespoons Vanilla Extract, Pure

- ½ Cup Oil
- 2 Cups Zucchini, Peeled & Grated

Directions:
4. Mix your cocoa, salt, flour, sugar and baking soda together.
5. Add in your oil, vanilla and zucchini, mixing well.
6. Bake at 350 in a nine by thirteen inch pan until done.

Interesting Facts: Zucchini: This commonly known vegetable (which botanically is considered a fruit!), promotes healthy eyes and heart function. They are high in folate and potassium. They are great to use as a substitute for spaghetti/noddles, just grab a spiralizer and get spiralizing!

Tofu Saag

Serves: 6

Time: 50 Minutes

Calories: 210

Protein: 12 Grams

Fat: 13.7 Grams

Carbs: 13 Grams

Ingredients:

- 21 Ounces Water Packed Tofu, Fir & Cubed into 1 Inch Pieces
- 10 Ounces Baby Spinach, Torn
- 2 Tablespoons Canola Oil, Divided
- 10 Ounces Baby Kale, Stemmed
- 1 Teaspoon Cumin
- 1 Teaspoon Fennel
- 8 Green Cardamom Pods
- 6 Whole Cloves
- 3 Red Chilies, Red

- 2 Tablespoon Ginger, Fresh & Minced
- Sea Salt to Tate
- 1 Teaspoon Water
- 1/8 Teaspoon Red Pepper

Directions:

1. Cook your tofu in two batches, making sure to drain it on paper towels. Your tofu should be golden.
2. Get out a Dutch oven and then bring two inches of water to a boil, adding in your kale and spinach. Cover and cook until wilted. This should take four minutes, and then stir occasionally. Drain well, and reserve the cooking liquid. Place your spinach and kale into a blender, and blend until smooth. Use your cooking liquid as needed to blend.
3. Combine a tablespoon of oil, a teaspoon of cumin seeds, fennel, and red chilies to a skillet. Cook for two minutes until golden brown and fragrant. Make sure to stir frequently.
4. Stir in your ginger, and cook for thirty seconds. Remove your cardamom and cloves, and then discard them.
5. Stir in your spinach, and then add a quarter cup of cooking liquid into a blender, making a puree. Scrape it down, and then put it in the pan. Stir in your salt, and then cook for five more minutes.
6. Put your tofu on top of your spinach mix, and then cover. Cook for another five more minutes.
7. Combine your ghee, cumin, fennel, and remaining red chilies. Before serving add teaspoon of water as you stir.

Interesting Facts: Spinach is one of the most superb green veggies out there. Each serving is packed with 3 grams of protein and is a highly encouraged component of the plant-based diet.

Pumpkin & Cinnamon Fudge

Serves: 25

Time: 2 Hours 10 Minutes

Calories: 110

Protein: 1.2 Grams

Fat: 10.63 Grams

Carbs: 5 Grams

Ingredients:

- 1 Teaspoon Ground Cinnamon
- 1 Cup Pumpkin Puree
- ¼ Teaspoon Nutmeg, Ground
- 1 ¾ Cup Coconut Butter, Melted
- 1 Tablespoon Coconut Oil

Directions:

1. Mix together your pumpkin, spices, coconut butter and coconut oil, whisking together.
2. Spread this mixture into a pan, and then cover it with foil. Press it down, and then discard the foil.
3. Refrigerate for two hours, and then chop into squares.

Interesting Facts: Pumpkin seeds are popularly known as a yummy snack, and can also be easily incorporated into soups, yogurt, salads, and more! They are loaded with iron, Vitamins C, E, and K, and essential omega-3s.

Oatmeal Sponge Cookies

Serves: 12

Time: 25 Minutes

Calories: 79.1

Protein: 2 Grams

Fat: 1 Gram

Carbs: 16.4 Grams

Ingredients:

- ¼ Cup Applesauce
- ½ Teaspoon Cinnamon
- 1/3 Cup Raisins
- ½ Teaspoon Vanilla Extract, Pure
- 1 Cup Ripe Banana, Mashed
- 2 Cups Oatmeal

Directions:
1. Start by heating your oven to 350.
2. Mix everything together. It should be gooey.
3. Drop it onto an ungreased baking sheet by the tablespoon, and then flatten.
4. Bake for fifteen minutes.

Interesting Facts: Cinnamon: This spice is an absolute powerhouse and is considered one of the healthiest, beneficial spices on the plant. It's widely known for its medicinal properties. This spice is loaded with powerful antioxidants and is popular for its anti-inflammatory properties. It can reduce heart disease and lower blood sugar levels.

Black Bean Dip

Serves: 2

Time: 10 Minutes

Calories: 190

Protein: 13 Grams

Fat: 1 Gram

Carbs: 35 Grams

Ingredients:

- 14 Ounces Black Beans, Drained & Rinsed
- 1 Lime, Juiced & Zested
- ¼ Cup Cilantro, Fresh & Chopped
- ¼ Cup Water
- 1 Teaspoon Cumin
- 1 Tablespoon Tamari
- Pinch Cayenne Pepper

Directions:

1. Process everything but your cilantro together until smooth, and then serve garnished with cilantro.

Interesting Facts: Oatmeal packed with B vitamins, zinc, magnesium, and protein. Bonus: They aid in digestion and assist with suppressing appetite, which aids in weight loss!

Kale Chips

Serves: 4

Time: 25 Minutes

Calories: 25.1

Protein: 1.7 Grams

Fat: 0.4 Grams

Carbs: 5 Grams

Ingredients:

- 1 Bunch Kale
- 1 Spritz Olive Oil

Directions:

1. Heat your oven to 250, and then wash your kale before patting it dry.
2. Arrange your kale on a prepared baking sheet, making sure your kale doesn't overlap. Spray it down with olive oil, and then season with salt.
3. Cook for twenty minutes.

Interesting Facts: Kale is the latest superfood of the Vegan world. It is a favorite when deciding to eliminate meat from your diet as it is very high in iron, vitamin K and potassium. It is also extremely high in fibre and vitamin A

Radish Chips

Serves: 4

Time: 20 Minutes

Calories: 3.6

Protein: 0.2 Grams

Fat: 0 Grams

Carbs: 0.8 Grams

Ingredients:

- 10-15 Radishes, Large
- Sea Salt & Black Pepper to Taste

Directions:

1. Start by heating your oven to 375.
2. Slice your radishes thin, and then spread them out on a cookie sheet that's been sprayed with cooking spray.
3. Mist the radishes with cooking spray, and then season with salt and pepper.
4. Bake for ten minutes, and then flip.
5. Bake for five to ten minutes more. They should be crispy.

Interesting Facts: Potatoes are a great starchy source of potassium and protein. They are pretty inexpensive if you are one that is watching their budget. Bonus: Very heart healthy!

Sautéed Pears

Serves: 6

Time: 35 Minutes

Calories: 220

Protein: 2 Grams

Fat: 10 Grams

Carbs: 31 Grams

Ingredients:

- 2 Tablespoons Margarine (Or Vegan Butter)
- ¼ Teaspoon Cinnamon
- ¼ Teaspoon Nutmeg
- 6 Bosc Pears, Peeled & Quartered
- 1 Tablespoon Lemon Juice
- ½ Cup Walnuts, Toasted & Chopped (Optional)

Directions:
1. Melt your vegan butter in a skillet, and then add your spices. Cook for a half a minute before adding in your pears.
2. Cook for fifteen minutes, and then stir in your lemon juice.
3. Serve with walnuts if desired.

Interesting Facts: Cinnamon: This spice is an absolute powerhouse and is considered one of the healthiest, beneficial spices on the plant. It's widely known for its medicinal properties. This spice is loaded with powerful antioxidants and is popular for its anti-inflammatory properties. It can reduce heart disease and lower blood sugar levels.

Pecan & Blueberry Crumble

Serves: 6

Time: 40 Minutes

Calories: 381

Protein: 10 Grams

Fat: 32 Grams

Net Carbs: 20 Grams

Ingredients:

- 14 Ounces Blueberries
- 1 Tablespoon Lemon Juice, Fresh
- 1 ½ Teaspoon Stevia Powder
- 3 Tablespoons Chia Seeds
- 2 Cups Almond Flour, Blanched
- ¼ Cup Pecans, Chopped
- 5 Tablespoon coconut Oil
- 2 Tablespoon Cinnamon

Directions:

1. Mix together your blueberries, stevia, chia seeds and lemon juice, and place it in an iron skillet.
2. Mix ingredients while spreading it over your blueberries.
3. Heat your oven to 400, and then transfer it to an oven safe skillet, baking for a half hour.

Interesting Facts: Blueberries: These guys are a delectable treat that is easily incorporated into many dishes. They are packed with antioxidants and Vitamin C. Bonus: Blueberries have been proven to promote eye health and slow macular degeneration.

Rice Pudding

Serves: 6

Time: 1 Hour 35 Minutes

Calories: 330

Protein: 5 Grams

Fat: 10 Grams

Carbs: 52 Grams

Ingredients:

- 1 Cup Brown Rice
- 1 Teaspoon Vanilla Extract, Pure
- ½ Teaspoon Sea Salt, Fine
- ½ Teaspoon Cinnamon
- ¼ Teaspoon Nutmeg

- 3 Egg Substitutes
- 3 Cups Coconut Milk, Light
- 2 Cups Brown Rice, Cooked

Directions:

3. Blend all of your ingredients together before pouring them into a two quarter dish.
4. Bake at 300 for ninety minutes before serving.

Interesting Facts: Brown rice is incredibly high in antioxidants and good vitamins. It's relative, 14 white rice is far less beneficial as much of these healthy nutrients get destroyed during the process of milling. You can also opt for red and black rice or wild rice. The meal options for this healthy grain are limitless!

Mango Sticky Rice

Serves: 3

Time: 35 Minutes

Calories: 571

Protein: 6 Grams

Fat: 29.6 Grams

Carbs: 77.6 Grams

Ingredients:

- ½ Cup Sugar
- 1 Mango, Sliced
- 14 Ounces Coconut Milk, Canned
- ½ Cup Basmati Rice

Directions:

1. Cook your rice per package instructions, and add half of your sugar. When cooking your rice, substitute half of your water for half of your coconut milk.
2. Boil your remaining coconut milk in a saucepan with your remaining sugar.
3. Boil on high heat until it's thick, and then add in your mango slices.

Interesting Facts: Mangos contain 50% of the daily Vitamin C you should consume which aid in bone and immune health.

Soup Salads And Sides

Cauliflower Coconut Rice

Total Time: 20 minutes

Serves: 3

Ingredients:

- 3 cups cauliflower rice
- ½ tsp onion powder
- 1 tsp chili paste
- 2/3 cup coconut milk
- Salt

Directions:

- Add all ingredients to the pan and heat over medium-low heat. Stir to combine.
- Cook for 10 minutes. Stir after every 2 minutes.
- Remove lid and cook until excess liquid absorbed.
- Serve and enjoy.

Nutritional Value (Amount per Serving): Calories 155; Fat 13.1 g; Carbohydrates 9.2 g; Sugar 4.8 g; Protein 3.4 g; Cholesterol 1 mg;

Fried Okra

Total Time: 20 minutes

Serves: 4

Ingredients:

- 1 lb fresh okra, cut into ¼" slices
- 1/3 cup almond meal
- Pepper
- Salt
- Oil for frying

Directions:

- Heat oil in large pan over medium-high heat.
- In a bowl, mix together sliced okra, almond meal, pepper, and salt until well coated.
- Once the oil is hot then add okra to the hot oil and cook until lightly browned.
- Remove fried okra from pan and allow to drain on paper towels.
- Serve and enjoy.

Nutritional Value (Amount per Serving): Calories 91; Fat 4.2 g; Carbohydrates 10.2 g; Sugar 10.2 g; Protein 3.9 g; Cholesterol 0 mg;

Asparagus Mash

Total Time: 20 minutes

Serves: 2

Ingredients:

- 10 asparagus shoots, chopped
- 1 tsp lemon juice
- 2 tbsp fresh parsley
- 2 tbsp coconut cream
- 1 small onion, diced
- 1 tbsp coconut oil
- Pepper
- Salt

Directions:

- Sauté onion in coconut oil until onion is softened.
- Blanch chopped asparagus in hot water for 2 minutes and drain immediately.
- Add sautéed onion, lemon juice, parsley, coconut cream, asparagus, pepper, and salt into the blender and blend until smooth.
- Serve warm and enjoy.

Nutritional Value (Amount per Serving): Calories 125; Fat 10.6 g; Carbohydrates 7.5 g; Sugar 3.6 g; Protein 2.6 g; Cholesterol 0 mg;

Baked Asparagus

Total Time: 25 minutes

Serves: 4

Ingredients:

- 40 asparagus spears
- 2 tbsp vegetable seasoning
- 2 tbsp garlic powder
- 2 tbsp salt

Directions:

- Preheat the oven to 450 F/ 232 C.
- Arrange all asparagus spears on baking tray and season with vegetable seasoning, garlic powder, and salt.
- Place in preheated oven and bake for 20 minutes.
- Serve warm and enjoy.

Nutritional Value (Amount per Serving): Calories 75; Fat 0.9 g; Carbohydrates 13.5 g; Sugar 5.5 g; Protein 6.7 g; Cholesterol 0 mg;

Spinach with Coconut Milk

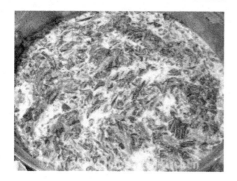

Total Time: 25 minutes

Serves: 6

Ingredients:

- 16 oz spinach
- 2 tsp curry powder
- 13.5 oz coconut milk
- 1 tsp lemon zest
- ½ tsp salt

Directions:

- Add spinach in pan and heat over medium heat. Once it is hot then add curry paste and few tablespoons of coconut milk. Stir well.
- Add remaining coconut milk, lemon zest, and salt and cook until thickened.
- Serve and enjoy.

Nutritional Value (Amount per Serving): Calories 167; Fat 15.6 g; Carbohydrates 6.7 g; Sugar 2.5 g; Protein 3.7 g; Cholesterol 0 mg;

Delicious Cabbage Steaks

Total Time: 1 hour 10 minutes

Serves: 6

Ingredients:

- 1 medium cabbage head, slice 1" thick
- 2 tbsp olive oil
- 1 tbsp garlic, minced
- Pepper
- Salt

Directions:

- In a small bowl, mix together garlic and olive oil.
- Brush garlic and olive oil mixture onto both sides of sliced cabbage.
- Season cabbage slices with pepper and salt.
- Place cabbage slices onto a baking tray and bake at 350 F/ 180 C for 1 hour. Turn after 30 minutes.
- Serve and enjoy.

Nutritional Value (Amount per Serving): Calories 72; Fat 4.8 g; Carbohydrates 7.4 g; Sugar 3.8 g; Protein 1.6 g; Cholesterol 0 mg;

Garlic Zucchini Squash

Total Time: 20 minutes

Serves: 4

Ingredients:

- 1 small squash, sliced
- 2 tbsp fresh basil, chopped
- 2 tbsp olive oil
- 1 garlic clove, chopped
- 1 large onion, sliced
- 2 fresh tomatoes, cut into wedges
- 1 small zucchini, sliced
- Pepper
- Salt

Directions:

- Heat olive oil in a pan over medium-high heat.
- Add onion, squash, zucchini, and garlic and sauté until lightly brown.
- Add basil and tomatoes and cook for 5 minutes. Season with pepper and salt.
- Simmer over low heat until squash is tender.
- Stir well and serve.

Nutritional Value (Amount per Serving): Calories 97; Fat 7.2 g; Carbohydrates 8.2 g; Sugar 4.4 g; Protein 1.4 g; Cholesterol 0 mg;

Tomato Avocado Cucumber Salad

Total Time: 10 minutes

Serves: 4

Ingredients:

- 1 cucumber, sliced
- 2 avocado, chopped
- ½ onion, sliced
- 2 tomatoes, chopped
- 1 bell pepper, chopped
- For dressing:
- 2 tbsp cilantro
- ¼ tsp garlic powder
- 2 tbsp olive oil
- 1 tbsp lemon juice
- ½ tsp black pepper
- ½ tsp salt

Directions:

- In a small bowl, mix together all dressing ingredients and set aside.
- Add all salad ingredients into the large mixing bowl and mix well.
- Pour dressing over salad and toss well.
- Serve immediately and enjoy.

Nutritional Value (Amount per Serving): Calories 130; Fat 9.8 g; Carbohydrates 10.6 g; Sugar 5.1 g; Protein 2.1 g; Cholesterol 0 mg;

Cabbage Coconut Salad

Total Time: 15 minutes

Serves: 4

Ingredients:

- 1/3 cup unsweetened desiccated coconut
- ½ medium head cabbage, shredded
- 2 tsp sesame seeds
- ¼ cup tamari sauce
- ¼ cup olive oil
- 1 fresh lemon juice
- ½ tsp cumin
- ½ tsp curry powder
- ½ tsp ginger powder

Directions:

- Add all ingredients into the large mixing bowl and toss well.
- Place salad bowl in refrigerator for 1 hour.
- Serve and enjoy.

Nutritional Value (Amount per Serving): Calories 197; Fat 16.6 g; Carbohydrates 11.4 g; Sugar 7.1 g; Protein 3.5 g; Cholesterol 0 mg;

Asian Cucumber Salad

Total Time: 10 minutes

Serves: 6

Ingredients:

- 4 cups cucumbers, sliced
- ¼ tsp red pepper flakes
- ½ tsp sesame oil
- 1 tsp sesame seeds
- ¼ cup rice wine vinegar
- ¼ cup red pepper, diced
- ¼ cup onion, sliced
- ½ tsp sea salt

Directions:

- Add all ingredients into the mixing bowl and toss well.
- Serve immediately and enjoy.

Nutritional Value (Amount per Serving): **Calories 27; Fat 0.7 g; Carbohydrates 3.5 g; Sugar 1.6 g; Protein 0.7 g; Cholesterol 0 mg;**

Mexican Cauliflower Rice

Total Time: 25 minutes

Serves: 4

Ingredients:

- 1 medium cauliflower head, cut into florets
- ½ cup tomato sauce
- ¼ tsp black pepper
- 1 tsp chili powder
- 2 garlic cloves, minced
- ½ medium onion, diced
- 1 tbsp coconut oil
- ½ tsp sea salt

Directions:

- Add cauliflower florets into the food processor and process until it looks like rice.
- Heat oil in a pan over medium-high heat.
- Add onion to the pan and sauté for 5 minutes or until softened.

- Add garlic and cook for 1 minute.
- Add cauliflower rice, chili powder, pepper, and salt. Stir well.
- Add tomato sauce and cook for 5 minutes.
- Stir well and serve warm.

Nutritional Value (Amount per Serving): Calories 83; Fat 3.7g; Carbohydrates 11.5 g; Sugar 5.4 g; Protein 3.6 g; Cholesterol 0 mg; ;

Turnip Salad

Total Time: 10 minutes

Serves: 4

Ingredients:

- 4 white turnips, spiralized
- 1 lemon juice
- 4 dill sprigs, chopped
- 2 tbsp olive oil
- 1 1/2 tsp salt

Directions:

- Season spiralized turnip with salt and gently massage with hands.
- Add lemon juice and dill. Season with pepper and salt.
- Drizzle with olive oil and combine everything well.
- Serve immediately and enjoy.

Nutritional Value (Amount per Serving): Calories 49; Fat 1.1 g; Carbohydrates 9 g; Sugar 5.2 g; Protein 1.4 g; Cholesterol 0 mg;

Brussels sprouts Salad

Total Time: 20 minutes

Serves: 6

Ingredients:

- 1 ½ lbs Brussels sprouts, trimmed
- ¼ cup toasted hazelnuts, chopped
- 2 tsp Dijon mustard
- 1 ½ tbsp lemon juice
- 2 tbsp olive oil
- Pepper
- Salt

Directions:

- In a small bowl, whisk together oil, mustard, lemon juice, pepper, and salt.
- In a large bowl, combine together Brussels sprouts and hazelnuts.
- Pour dressing over salad and toss well.
- **Serve immediately and enjoy.**

Nutritional Value (Amount per Serving): Calories 111; Fat 7.1 g; Carbohydrates 11 g; Sugar 2.7 g; Protein 4.4 g; Cholesterol 0 mg;

Tomato Eggplant Spinach Salad

Total Time: 30 minutes

Serves: 4

Ingredients:

- 1 large eggplant, cut into 3/4 inch slices
- 5 oz spinach
- 1 tbsp sun-dried tomatoes, chopped
- 1 tbsp oregano, chopped
- 1 tbsp parsley, chopped
- 1 tbsp fresh mint, chopped
- 1 tbsp shallot, chopped
- For dressing:
- 1/4 cup olive oil
- 1/2 lemon juice
- 1/2 tsp smoked paprika
- 1 tsp Dijon mustard
- 1 tsp tahini

- 2 garlic cloves, minced
- Pepper
- Salt

Directions:

- Place sliced eggplants into the large bowl and sprinkle with salt and set aside for minutes.
- In a small bowl mix together all dressing ingredients. Set aside.
- Heat grill to medium-high heat.
- In a large bowl, add shallot, sun-dried tomatoes, herbs, and spinach.
- Rinse eggplant slices and pat dry with paper towel.
- Brush eggplant slices with olive oil and grill on medium high heat for 3-4 minutes on each side.
- Let cool the grilled eggplant slices then cut into quarters.
- Add eggplant to the salad bowl and pour dressing over salad. Toss well.
- Serve and enjoy.

Nutritional Value (Amount per Serving): Calories 163; Fat 13 g; Carbohydrates 10 g; Sugar 3 g; Protein 2 g; Cholesterol 0 mg;

Cauliflower Radish Salad

Total Time: 15 minutes

Serves: 4

Ingredients:

- 12 radishes, trimmed and chopped
- 1 tsp dried dill
- 1 tsp Dijon mustard
- 1 tbsp cider vinegar
- 1 tbsp olive oil
- 1 cup parsley, chopped
- ½ medium cauliflower head, trimmed and chopped
- ½ tsp black pepper
- ¼ tsp sea salt

Directions:

- In a mixing bowl, combine together cauliflower, parsley, and radishes.
- In a small bowl, whisk together olive oil, dill, mustard, vinegar, pepper, and salt.
- Pour dressing over salad and toss well.
- Serve immediately and enjoy.

Nutritional Value (Amount per Serving): Calories 58; Fat 3.8 g; Carbohydrates 5.6 g; Sugar 2.1 g; Protein 2.1 g; Cholesterol 0 mg;

Celery Salad

Total Time: 10 minutes

Serves: 6

Ingredients:

- 6 cups celery, sliced
- ¼ tsp celery seed
- 1 tbsp lemon juice
- 2 tsp lemon zest, grated
- 1 tbsp parsley, chopped
- 1 tbsp olive oil
- Sea salt

Directions:

- Add all ingredients into the large mixing bowl and toss well.
- Serve immediately and enjoy.

Nutritional Value (Amount per Serving): Calories 38; Fat 2.5 g; Carbohydrates 3.3 g; Sugar 1.5 g; Protein 0.8 g; Cholesterol 0 mg;

Ginger Avocado Kale Salad

Total Time: 15 minutes

Serves: 4

Ingredients:

- 1 avocado, peeled and sliced
- 1 tbsp ginger, grated
- 1/2 lb kale, chopped
- 1/4 cup parsley, chopped
- 2 fresh scallions, chopped

Directions:

- Add all ingredients into the mixing bowl and toss well.
- Serve and enjoy.

Nutritional Value (Amount per Serving): Calories 139; Fat 9.9 g; Carbohydrates 12 g; Sugar 0.5 g; Protein 3 g; Cholesterol 0 mg;

Avocado Cabbage Salad

Total Time: 20 minutes

Serves: 4

Ingredients:

- 2 avocados, diced
- 4 cups cabbage, shredded
- 3 tbsp fresh parsley, chopped
- 2 tbsp apple cider vinegar
- 4 tbsp olive oil
- 1 cup cherry tomatoes, halved
- 1/2 tsp pepper
- 1 1/2 tsp sea salt

Directions:

- Add cabbage, avocados, and tomatoes to a medium bowl and mix well.
- In a small bowl, whisk together oil, parsley, vinegar, pepper, and salt.
- Pour dressing over vegetables and mix well.
- Serve and enjoy.

Nutritional Value (Amount per Serving): Calories 253; Fat 21.6 g; Carbohydrates 14 g; Sugar 4 g; Protein 3.5 g; Cholesterol 0 mg;

Vegetable Salad

Total Time: 15 minutes

Serves: 6

Ingredients:

- 2 cups cauliflower florets
- 2 cups carrots, chopped
- 2 cups cherry tomatoes, halved
- 2 tbsp shallots, minced
- 1 bell pepper, seeded and chopped
- 1 cucumber, seeded and chopped
- For dressing:
- 2 garlic cloves, minced
- 1/2 cup red wine vinegar
- 1/2 cup olive oil
- Pepper
- Salt

Directions:

- In a small bowl, combine together all dressing ingredients.
- Add all salad ingredients to the large bowl and toss well.
- Pour dressing over salad and toss well.
- Place salad bowl in refrigerator for 4 hours.
- Serve chilled and enjoy.

Nutritional Value (Amount per Serving): Calories 200; Fat 17.1 g; Carbohydrates 12.1 g; Sugar 6.1 g; Protein 2.2 g; Cholesterol 0 mg;

Refreshing Cucumber Salad

Total Time: 10 minutes

Serves: 4

Ingredients:

- 1/3 cup cucumber basil ranch
- 1 cucumber, chopped
- 3 tomatoes, chopped
- 3 tbsp fresh herbs, chopped
- ½ onion, sliced

Directions:

- Add all ingredients into the large mixing bowl and toss well.
- Serve immediately and enjoy.

Nutritional Value (Amount per Serving): Calories 84; Fat 3.4 g; Carbohydrates 12.5 g; Sugar 6.8 g; Protein 2 g; Cholesterol 0 mg;

Avocado Almond Cabbage Salad

Total Time: 15 minutes

Serves: 3

Ingredients:

- 3 cups savoy cabbage, shredded
- ½ cup blanched almonds
- 1 avocado, chopped
- ¼ tsp pepper
- ¼ tsp sea salt
- For dressing:
- 1 tsp coconut aminos
- ½ tsp Dijon mustard
- 1 tbsp lemon juice
- 3 tbsp olive oil
- Pepper
- Salt

Directions:

- In a small bowl, mix together all dressing ingredients and set aside.
- Add all salad ingredients to the large bowl and mix well.
- Pour dressing over salad and toss well.
- Serve immediately and enjoy.

Nutritional Value (Amount per Serving): Calories 317; Fat 14.1 g; Carbohydrates 39.8 g; Sugar 9.3 g; Protein 11.6 g; Cholesterol 0 mg;

Drinks and dessert

Avocado Pudding

Total Time: 10 minutes

Serves: 8

Ingredients:

- 2 ripe avocados, peeled, pitted and cut into pieces
- 1 tbsp fresh lime juice
- 14 oz can coconut milk
- 80 drops of liquid stevia
- 2 tsp vanilla extract

Directions:

- Add all ingredients into the blender and blend until smooth.
- Serve and enjoy.

Nutritional Value (Amount per Serving): Calories 317; Fat 30.1 g; Carbohydrates 9.3 g; Sugar 0.4 g; Protein 3.4 g; Cholesterol 0 mg;

Almond Butter Brownies

Total Time: 30 minutes

Serves: 4

Ingredients:

- 1 scoop protein powder
- 2 tbsp cocoa powder
- 1/2 cup almond butter, melted
- 1 cup bananas, overripe

Directions:

- Preheat the oven to 350 F/ 176 C.
- Spray brownie tray with cooking spray.
- Add all ingredients into the blender and blend until smooth.
- Pour batter into the prepared dish and bake in preheated oven for 20 minutes.
- Serve and enjoy.

Nutritional Value (Amount per Serving): Calories 82; Fat 2.1 g; Carbohydrates 11.4 g; Protein 6.9 g; Sugars 5 g; Cholesterol 16 mg;

Raspberry Chia Pudding

Total Time: 3 hours 10 minutes

Serves: 2

Ingredients:

- 4 tbsp chia seeds
- 1 cup coconut milk
- 1/2 cup raspberries

Directions:

- Add raspberry and coconut milk in a blender and blend until smooth.
- Pour mixture into the Mason jar.
- Add chia seeds in a jar and stir well.
- Close jar tightly with lid and shake well.
- Place in refrigerator for 3 hours.
- Serve chilled and enjoy.

Nutritional Value (Amount per Serving): Calories 361; Fat 33.4 g; Carbohydrates 13.3 g; Sugar 5.4 g; Protein 6.2 g; Cholesterol 0 mg;

Chocolate Fudge

Total Time: 10 minutes

Serves: 12

Ingredients:

- 4 oz unsweetened dark chocolate
- 3/4 cup coconut butter
- 15 drops liquid stevia
- 1 tsp vanilla extract

Directions:

- Melt coconut butter and dark chocolate.
- Add ingredients to the large bowl and combine well.
- Pour mixture into a silicone loaf pan and place in refrigerator until set.
- Cut into pieces and serve.

Nutritional Value (Amount per Serving): Calories 157; Fat 14.1 g; Carbohydrates 6.1 g; Sugar 1 g; Protein 2.3 g; Cholesterol 0 mg;

Quick Chocó Brownie

Total Time: 10 minutes

Serves: 1

Ingredients:

- 1/4 cup almond milk
- 1 tbsp cocoa powder
- 1 scoop chocolate protein powder
- 1/2 tsp baking powder

Directions:

- In a microwave-safe mug blend together baking powder, protein powder, and cocoa.
- Add almond milk in a mug and stir well.
- Place mug in microwave and microwave for 30 seconds.
- Serve and enjoy.

Nutritional Value (Amount per Serving): Calories 207; Fat 15.8 g; Carbohydrates 9.5 g; Sugar 3.1 g; Protein 12.4 g; Cholesterol 20 mg;

Simple Almond Butter Fudge

Total Time: 15 minutes

Serves: 8

Ingredients:

- 1/2 cup almond butter
- 15 drops liquid stevia
- 2 1/2 tbsp coconut oil

Directions:

- Combine together almond butter and coconut oil in a saucepan. Gently warm until melted.
- Add stevia and stir well.
- Pour mixture into the candy container and place in refrigerator until set.
- Serve and enjoy.

Nutritional Value (Amount per Serving): Calories 43; Fat 4.8 g; Carbohydrates 0.2 g; Protein 0.2 g; Sugars 0 g; Cholesterol 0 mg

Coconut Peanut Butter Fudge

Total Time: 1 hour 15 minutes

Serves: 20

Ingredients:

- 12 oz smooth peanut butter
- 3 tbsp coconut oil
- 4 tbsp coconut cream
- 15 drops liquid stevia
- Pinch of salt

Directions:

- Line baking tray with parchment paper.
- Melt coconut oil in a saucepan over low heat.
- Add peanut butter, coconut cream, stevia, and salt in a saucepan. Stir well.
- Pour fudge mixture into the prepared baking tray and place in refrigerator for 1 hour.
- Cut into pieces and serve.

Nutritional Value (Amount per Serving): Calories 125; Fat 11.3 g; Carbohydrates 3.5 g; Sugar 1.7 g; Protein 4.3 g; Cholesterol 0 mg;

Lemon Mousse

Total Time: 10 minutes

Serves: 2

Ingredients:

- 14 oz coconut milk
- 12 drops liquid stevia
- 1/2 tsp lemon extract
- 1/4 tsp turmeric

Directions:

- Place coconut milk can in the refrigerator for overnight. Scoop out thick cream into a mixing bowl.
- Add remaining ingredients to the bowl and whip using a hand mixer until smooth.
- Transfer mousse mixture to a zip-lock bag and pipe into small serving glasses. Place in refrigerator.
- Serve chilled and enjoy.

Nutritional Value (Amount per Serving): Calories 444; Fat 45.7 g; Carbohydrates 10 g; Sugar 6 g; Protein 4.4 g; Cholesterol 0 mg;

Chocó Chia Pudding

Total Time: 10 minutes

Serves: 6

Ingredients:

- 2 1/2 cups coconut milk
- 2 scoops stevia extract powder
- 6 tbsp cocoa powder
- 1/2 cup chia seeds
- 1/2 tsp vanilla extract
- 1/8 cup xylitol
- 1/8 tsp salt

Directions:

- Add all ingredients into the blender and blend until smooth.
- Pour mixture into the glass container and place in refrigerator.
- Serve chilled and enjoy.

Nutritional Value (Amount per Serving): Calories 259; Fat 25.4 g; Carbohydrates 10.2 g; Sugar 3.5 g; Protein 3.8 g; Cholesterol 0 mg;

Chapter 8 21-Day Meal Plan

DAYS	BREAKFAST	MAIN DISHES	SNACKS/DESSERTS
1.	Keto Porridge	burgers	Coconut Peanut Butter Fudge
2.	Easy Chia Seed Pudding	Grilled Eggplant Steaks	Pumpkin & Cinnamon Fudge
3.	Cinnamon Noatmeal	Cauliflower Rice Tabbouleh	Black Bean Dip
4.	Delicious Vegan Zoodles	Dijon Maple Burgers	Zucchini Brownies
5.	Avocado Tofu Scramble	Cauliflower Steaks	Tofu Saag
6.	Chia Raspberry Pudding Shots	bowl	Kale Chips
7.	Healthy Chia-Almond Pudding	hummus	Pecan & Blueberry Crumble
8.	Delicious Tofu Fries	Pesto & Tomato Quinoa	Sautéed Pears
9.	Almond	Summer	Rice Pudding

	Coconut Porridge	Chickpea Salad	
10.	Avocado Breakfast Smoothie	Corn & Black Bean Salad	Mango Sticky Rice
11.	Protein Breakfast Shake	Fruity Kale Salad	Oatmeal Sponge Cookies
12.	Avocado Chocó Cinnamon Smoothie	Spinach & Orange Salad	Radish Chips
13.	Strawberry Chia Matcha Pudding	Edamame Salad	Avocado Pudding
14.	Chia Cinnamon Smoothie	spaghetti	Raspberry Chia Pudding
15.	Vegetable Tofu Scramble	Cauliflower Rice Tabbouleh	Chocó Chia Pudding
16.	Healthy Breakfast Granola	Olive & Fennel Salad	Coconut Peanut Butter Fudge
17.	Apple Avocado	Ratatouille	Lemon Mousse

	Coconut Smoothie		
18.	Fresh Berries with Cream	fried vegetables	Quick Chocó Brownie
19.	Almond Hemp Heart Porridge	fajitas	Chocolate Fudge
20.	Grain-free Overnight Oats	tofu	Simple Almond Butter Fudge
21.	Healthy Spinach Green Smoothie	Baked Okra & Tomato	Almond Butter Brownies

Conclusion

There are so many diets in today's society that can be beneficial to our minds, bodies, and health. One of the most popular diets that people transition to is being a vegan. As with any diet you choose, you should consult your doctor and find out if it is safe for you. In this book, we're going to give you vital information about this diet to help give you more information as well. It may be for animal rights, the planet, or maybe they just want to get healthier. Some also have religious, moral, or ethical reasoning behind their decision to be vegan. There are many benefits to adopting this lifestyle but the first thing we need to understand is what is a vegan? A vegan is someone who does not eat or use animal products. This means you need to cut out a lot of things you take for granted such as milk, eggs, cheese, honey, butter and more. Of course, one of the obvious things about a vegan diet is no meat of any kind. You'll have to rethink your dairy, meal plans, even the makeup and clothes you wear or the shampoo you use for your hair. This means you will have to either keep them out altogether from your life or replace them with vegan-friendly options. With so many people turning toward veganism, it's been said that it's turned into a movement by many articles and even some news stations, companies are listening and making amazing new products that are vegan-friendly thereby making it easier than ever to adopt this lifestyle and reap the benefits.

There is really only one way to be a vegan as opposed to other diets where they have subsections and other variations. However, while the definition of being a vegan is solid, there are many different ways to exact a vegan diet. Many have pros and cons and it's up to you to determine which one is the best for your issues and health. It's also important to do your research because some of the diets that claim to be vegan are not because they add meat and dairy into the diet later on after the first few weeks. This is obviously not a vegan diet and therefore not recommended for the changes you're trying to make in your lifestyle.

Some of the most popular vegan diets that people have either been wanting to try or have been curious about are the 'raw till four diet' which has been made amazingly popular due to a vegan on a viral video site. As of now, I believe there is a following of about eight thousand or more, plant-based vegan. Most of the people that use this diet have said that they've tried others, and this was the best for them; low carb vegan such as keto or paleo; and the engine two diets on the opposite side of keto. Some prefer high carb low-fat diets, the detox vegan diet, or even the junk food vegan diet which they love because it proves that being a vegan doesn't have to just stick to healthy 'boring' food but instead can eat amazingly tasty food as well.

One of the most obvious benefits of veganism is that they tend to be skinnier and able to better maintain a healthier weight than most meat eaters. As with any diet, this depends on what you eat. There are many meat and cheese substitutes that are vegan, but some can be high in calories and other things that can make you gain weight if that's all you're eating or junk food related items. Many companies are understanding that more people are becoming vegan and therefore want to put out substitutes and many people fill up on these because they don't do the proper research as to how they should be eating. This causes weight gain. Another problem for new vegans is they listen to fad diet people. An example of this is viral video sites. A lot of the information from these videos is solid and well informed; others, not so much.

There have been people on these channels telling people to eat over five thousand calories a day in fruit and only to exercise an hour. Obviously, this may not be the best advice because that's far too much sugar and calories with only one hour of exercise. You wouldn't be able to burn off that many calories with so little work out time. This could make you balloon up and have a host of health issues. Another fad diet that has come under scrutiny is the 'raw till four' simply because nutritionists have said it's dangerous especially if you're following some of the people on these viral video sites especially when they take it to some of the far extremes. So it's important to know what it is you're doing with your diet. Eating properly can make a vegan skinnier; eating improperly will not.

Since you will no longer be eating meat or dairy, you are likely to be eating foods with a lot less saturated fat. Saturated fat is linked to high cholesterol and increased risk of heart disease. Lower blood pressure is another great benefit of cutting animal products out of your life.

Made in the USA
Monee, IL
26 December 2019